CAN YOU
BE A
HYPNOTIST?

How to Create a Fulfilling and Lucrative Career Helping
People with Modern and Professional Hypnosis

BY ERIKA FLINT, BCH, OB

Cover Design: Jennifer Stimson
Editing: Moriah Howell
Author's photo courtesy of: Dawn Matthes

Too many people, who just want to help others, are doing too many things that just don't work. So, I am super excited for everyone to learn about modern hypnosis and Erika does a great job launching it into mainstream consciousness. Well done, Erika.

— **Celeste Hackett**

Can You be a Hypnotist by Erika Flint is an easy to understand, science-based, practical manual, which everyone who wants to help others should read. Me being a scientist and board certified hypnotist myself, I find this book very valuable and immensely inspiring to those who want to join us in our highly rewarding profession or want to add an incredible skill to their toolbox to serve clients.

— **Petra Frese, author of "Overcome Your Devastating Diagnosis - Script for Hope"**

Yes, Yes, Yes! Erika perfectly described hypnosis and the process that helps clients make the changes they want. I loved the formula that is presented to use with each client, while personalized it for the individual, all done at the same time.

— **Deb Kizilcan BA. LMT. CCH**

Not only was this book the deciding factor in my question of whether to become a hypnotist, but it has served as a trusty reference guide time and again during my early months of hypnotist training. I often go back and reread some of the Professional Hypnotist Truth sections and I have some of them copied down and pinned to my vision board to help me stay in my center. I highly recommend it.

— **Victoria**

Erika Flint's latest book, *Can You Be a Hypnotist?*, may be aimed at those contemplating the profession, however, it is also helpful reading for hypnotists already in practice. One could easily change the title to Can You Be a Better Hypnotist?, for the book is full of the author's wisdom, encouraging ideas, provoking points, case study experiences and more. Reading this book sparked numerous new thoughts for me. As well, it provided reminders for hypnosis sessions with clients. Upon finishing the book, I found myself eagerly rereading Ms. Flint's 24 "Professional Hypnotist Truth(s)."*Can You Be a Hypnotist?* is absolutely loaded with important information. Compliments to Erika Flint, for this useful book!
 — Deborah Quigley, MS, CCH, Hypnotic Solutions, Rocky Point, NY

This book is part instructional, part inspirational and 110% practical. Not only is it clearly and cleanly written, the organizational layout of the document flowed easily to have the content make perfect sense. Each section builds on the previous with examples and case studies that "just fit." Great as a starter book for the beginner/ aspiring hypnotist or a check in for someone a little further along.
 — Lynne Potter Lord

If you have always felt compelled to help others and weren't sure how you wanted to go about doing so, then this book is a must read. It doesn't take years of study and tens of thousands of dollars to help people facilitate positive change in their lives. Hypnosis professionals help clients every day. Most people only know what they see on TV about hypnosis, and Erika lays out a clear explanation of hypnosis that dispels all of the myth and mystery about the process. The case studies she provides throughout the book demonstrate that hypnosis is about more than just quitting smoking and weight loss. An unfortunate hidden truth is the power of the human mind to work out its own problems—because each of us know deep in our subconscious exactly what we need to feel content and whole. Hypnotists guide clients into tapping in to this ability to create change in their lives. As a result, clients experience insights that change the way they see themselves and interact with the world around them. Becoming a Hypnosis Professional provides the opportunity to guide clients through transformation. If you are now considering training as a hypnosis professional, this guide will prove invaluable.

— *Penny Chiasson, CRNA, BCH, CPHI*

Wow, this book has everything you need to know to decide whether you can be a hypnotist. Actually, this book will make you WANT to be a hypnotist! Erika covers all the issues and questions you may have if you are interested in this field, but haven't yet taken the plunge. I have looked into becoming a hypnotist a lot, I have searched the internet, and googled many sources and there was always something lacking, and that gave me pause. Should I become a hypnotist? But, this book is the first time I was sure I got the whole picture, and I was convinced. I am so glad I read this book. I can't wait to take my first hypnotism class!

— *Kimberly Lorenz*

I truly enjoyed Erica Flint's book, *Can You be a Hypnotist?* It introduced the basic principles of hypnotherapy and explained them clearly. I see this book as a powerful agent for positive change. I would recommend it to anyone curious about becoming a hypnotist.

— *Kestral Garcia*

I love, love, love this book. I wish this was available for me before I started my training. It really introduces you to the new language of hypnosis before the classes start. I am a practicing hypnotist and have learned some great tips from this book and it is also reassuring to know that I am staying up to date with the newest practices. Thank you for allowing me to preview your wonderful book.

— *Lori Nelson LPN, CHT*

In *Can You Be a Hypnotist?*, Erika Flint shares her journey to become a full time hypnotist and inspires the reader to join her in this fulfilling and rewarding career. Erika combines her story well with what it means to be a hypnotist, what it takes to be a hypnotist, and using hypnotic techniques, she guides the reader as they step into the future, creating a blueprint for themselves as a future hypnotist. We often say in the hypnosis community "this is what I wish I would have had (or known) back when I was getting started, and it is absolutely true for this book. If you are considering a career change and hypnosis is one of your options, this is the book for you!

— Brenda Titus, Board Certified Hypnotist

This book is full of useful information - for the aspiring hypnotist and seasoned hypnotist alike! Flint's passion for the profession is inspiring.

— Diane Ripper

This book is as uplifting as it is practical. It certainly exceeded my expectations, especially the chapters on business skills and avoiding common mistakes. To learn those lessons the hard way would probably take a person many painful years, and it might cause some people to give up entirely. But the author provides generous insights, personal examples and remedies to help the reluctant hypnotist find their footing and thrive in what seems by many measures to be a growing and lucrative field. I'm thrilled I came across this book as it has further ignited my passion for hypnosis and actually making it a reality for me as a career for my future of helping people.

— Matthew B

Can You Be a Hypnotist? by Erika Flint tackles complex insights on hypnosis and the neuroscience behind it, with a thoughtful and seamless read. The book shines light on the beauty of hypnosis and how it can bring about true alignment (mind, body, and spirit) quickly. This book shows that we have the ability and power to better ourselves and that Hypnosis is just the tool that can break through barriers and walls. Erika is a dynamic speaker and author and this book will empower any person on the Hypnosis path!

— Robbie Ward

Well organized. Informative. Enlightening. And inspiring. *Can You Be A Hypnotist?* is an easy, must read for anyone who is at all curious about the practice of Hypnosis.

— Paula Engles

For Paige with love.

TABLE OF CONTENTS

FOREWORD

Over 20 years ago I started on this great hypnotic adventure. As an authority in the profession of hypnotism it is wonderful to know that what I have taught has had such a profound effect on so many and it is particularly satisfying when someone like Erika Flint can take the essence of what I have both created and taught and bring it to an audience of those considering entering into our beloved profession of hypnosis. But it is more than just a distillation of what I have taught, Erika is a lifelong learner and will introduce you to ideas of her own that have come out of her experience as well as weaving in concepts from others to provide you with a balanced and insightful introduction to our profession.

Never before has there been a book exactly like this. In this book, Erika has written a concise introduction to our profession. However, this book goes far beyond its title and stated intent. It introduces you to the exact kind of advanced work we can do and how to build a hypnosis practice using those systems and techniques.

This book is not about how to become the average hypnotist, rather this book is an introduction to becoming one of the best of the best, a "Top 1% Hypnosis Professional".

Years ago, when I first met Erika, I recognized that she is smart, focused and was open to learning. She had already been very successful in the software engineering industry and now that she had turned her attention to hypnosis she decided to make a complete career change.

She "got it"! Erika understood how powerful hypnosis sessions conducted at the highest level can be and it excited her. She became a 5-PATH® Certified Hypnosis Professional who was ready to get to work immediately, started helping others, and then began to train others to do our powerful lifechanging kind of hypnosis that the Top 1% can do. She has become a truly outstanding instructor in our profession.

I did not just train and certify Erika and let her go. We kept in touch. I invited her to be interviewed on my podcast, Hypnosis Etc. It was podcast 375 and, in that interview, I had her share how she went about moving successfully from her old career to a new career in hypnosis while replacing her previous very substantial income. The interview went so well that I invited her to be a regular co-host on the Hypnosis, Etc. program and has made many such free hypnosis training video podcasts with me since that one. Over the years, I have mentored her and supported her as she went on to became a writer and speaker in the hypnosis profession.

Erika is a quick learner. She soaked up everything and continued to grow as we worked together creating each new video for the Hypnosis, Etc. podcasts program. She also grew because of her personal experiences that comes from implementing what she has learned by seeing clients, lots of clients. Then came the kind of learning that can only come by teaching as she became a leading trainer.

I am so happy to see that this book is available. It is the best book for those who want to be truly great professional hypnotists and want to get the "inside scoop" on what it takes to become one of the best in the profession.

Erika has done an excellent job of "cutting to the chase" and letting you in on how it is all done so that you can make an informed choice to come into our beloved profession as a highly skilled and trained hypnosis professional. She masterfully blends the concepts which are a part of 5-PATH®, 7th Path Self-Hypnosis®

and The Secret Language of Feelings® with her own insights and experiences and case histories. She gives you an overview of how these processes and techniques get real results with real clients. Erika also blends in wisdom from other sources as well.

As a teacher and practitioner in our beloved profession, one of the greatest sources of satisfaction as a professional, beyond the satisfaction of helping my clients is when I watch a student really understand and implement what she has learned, and then to take it one step further and pass that teaching on to others, as she does so well in this book, *Can You Be A Hypnotist?*

Read on and you will discover the rewards of doing this kind of high-level work, gain insights into the use of advanced techniques such as instant and rapid inductions, age regression, and more. No one should enter the profession without first reading this book.

Cal Banyan, MA

Board Certified Hypnotist
Master Certified Professional Hypnosis Instructor
Creator of the 5-PATH® System, 7th Path Self-Hypnosis® and author of the book, The Secret Language of Feelings
Coauthor with Gerald F. Kein of the book, Hypnosis and Hypnotherapy: Basic to Advanced Techniques for the Professional
www.CalBanyan.com

CHAPTER ONE

WHY BECOME A HYPNOTIST?

Hypnosis is all around us.

When we're captivated by movies or music, we are hypnotized, focusing only on certain perceptions and filtering out all others.

When we lose track of time while doing something we love, we are hypnotized, absorbed completely in the present moment.

When we're "in the zone," we are hypnotized, performing at our peak without allowing anxiety or fear to dampen our performance.

You've already been in hypnosis thousands of times in your life.

It is our ability to both focus on and filter out certain elements of our awareness. Sometimes we do this consciously and on purpose; other times, it is done automatically by what we have learned through experience.

It's the power to intentionally use those techniques to make changes to our underlying automatic responses.

Hypnosis is a normal and natural state of mind, and our brain's primary job is to keep us alive. We've learned strategies and behaviors to support that. We call those habits and beliefs. Hypnosis is an elemental part of that learning.

When we were young, we borrowed habits and beliefs of authority figures around us and later on believed them to be our truth.

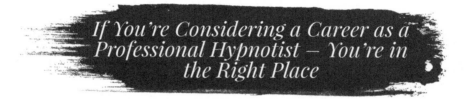

If You're Considering a Career as a Professional Hypnotist – You're in the Right Place

Later, we outgrow some of those old strategies and behaviors. We call them limiting beliefs and bad behaviors when they keep us stuck.

You're reading this book because you have an interest in learning hypnosis and possibly becoming a professional hypnotist. You're likely curious about the mind and the ability to affect change using advanced hypnosis techniques.

And you're in the right place.

You don't need to know anything about hypnosis or how it works to become a professional hypnotist. You will need to learn about hypnosis (and it's covered in Chapter 2).

You don't need any advanced training in psychotherapy, counselling, or neuroscience.

You may be feeling overwhelmed and not know where to start but want to learn more. You're not sure if you can make a living as a professional hypnotist. And you somehow found this book. Congratulations! You're in the right place. I'll be answering all of those questions and more throughout this book.

All you need to be a master hypnotist is the following three things:

1. A Servant's Heart
2. Willingness to learn the advanced techniques
3. Courage to do the hard work with clients – starting with yourself

A SERVANT'S HEART

You have a desire and willingness to help others. You may have such a strong desire to help others that it hurts. You see the suffering in the world, the pain it causes, the sadness and loneliness in the average person. You read articles about the constant bullying and abuse that is crippling so many people.

You may even have friends and family close to you with massive levels of anxiety and fear, with stories of neglect or abuse, with inabilities to sleep, who feel caught in endless cycles of barely making it from day to day.

You may notice how many people are turning towards substances, including alcohol, tobacco, and food, to help them feel better, only of course to discover the detrimental toll that lifestyle leads to over time.

And you may also have a personal story with hypnosis: how it helped you or a loved one or how you wished you had known about hypnosis earlier, before your loved one felt so alone or helpless.

You may currently be a coach, author, teacher, therapist, or nurse and help people every day with difficult issues. And you want to know, "Can hypnosis get me better results for those I am helping?"

WILLINGNESS TO LEARN THE ADVANCED TECHNIQUES

Hypnosis has changed in the last fifty years. We know so much more now about which hypnosis techniques actually work, the neuroscience behind the most effective techniques, and hypnotic language (including non-verbal communication) that is the most effective.

The good news is that these techniques can be learned. They are easy, and they take practice. Just as learning a new instrument requires daily practice, becoming a master hypnotist also take practice.

As a hypnotist, you use hypnosis to learn hypnosis. Hypnosis can help you read faster, learn quicker, and improve recall of the most important information. Hypnosis helps you focus and gain skill quickly.

COURAGE TO DO THE HARD WORK WITH CLIENTS – STARTING WITH YOURSELF FIRST!

The issues we help our clients with are not always easy

issues. Most of our clients have already tried to resolve their ssues with everything they already know, and it hasn't worked.

You have to be willing to do the necessary work with clients to help them overcome their fear and limiting beliefs and to create an environment for them to grow and change.

The first person I want you to do that with is yourself. The best hypnotists are true believers in hypnosis, and they have their own hypnosis experience. This doesn't mean you need to have it now before reading this book, but I hope you are willing to work on yourself and release any of your own limiting beliefs and negative self-talk and use the techniques in this book, as it will certainly help you to help your clients do the same.

The World Needs More Excellent Hypnotists

I am so happy that you picked up this book. The world needs more excellent hypnotists. Hypnotists with the right training who can help clients understand that the power is within them, with the advanced skills to help clients experience relief from anxiety in real time, with the heart-centered skills to truly listen, who then use that information to help clients find relief by the time they leave the office in a single session.

You don't have to be ready. You just have to be willing to take the next step, even if you're nervous about your ability to be good at it. Most hypnotists are – at first. And all that means is that they care. They care about their clients and want to do a good job. If that's you, keep reading.

Imagine That It Is Exactly One Year from Today

You are sitting in your office across from your client, a middle-aged woman who originally came to see you because she couldn't sleep. Her restless nights were causing multiple issues in her life, including low motivation, falling asleep at work, and over-eating.

You noticed when she arrived today that she looked visibly different – younger in fact. With a smile on her face, she tells you she's been sleeping again, and she's had the most peaceful and happy week of her life.

She looks directly at you, and states, "Thank you; you changed my life."

You feel at peace. You know the work you did with her was meaningful. It positively impacted her life. A deep sense of gratitude and happiness washes over you.

You feel content and excited for your client and for your business. And after your client leaves, you prepare for your next session, with another client who needs help with a different issue.

In a moment of reflection between clients, you think, "This is so much better than I ever thought."

The journey that brought you here over the past year has been both challenging and rewarding. You've learned so much about yourself, having your own business, and helping others. Looking back, you wouldn't change a thing – except maybe starting earlier.

You are a professional hypnotist. You have a thriving practice helping clients with a variety of issues: everyday issues and complex issue, issues they can't seem to resolve themselves using their best tools.

You have grown professionally and personally as well — you're able to do things in your life you once weren't able to. Your relationships have improved; it's easier for you to focus and get work accomplished, and you're healthier because you're using your own tools as a hypnotist to improve your own life.

My Story of Becoming a Professional Hypnotist

Hi, I'm Erika Flint. I am honored and grateful that you're reading this book. I'm an award-winning professional hypnotist and hypnotherapy instructor. I teach compassionate individuals to become professional hypnotists — and most of them have no or very little hypnosis experience to begin with. In 2012, I was working for one of the largest computing organizations in the world as a software engineer. I had no plans of becoming a hypnotist, nor did I know what hypnosis really was.

If you asked me back then what hypnosis was, I would have said it's something at the fair or similar to what a magician does. And I would have been right on both accounts but not entirely. The Truth About Hypnosis is revealed in Chapter 2. For now, just know that the forms of hypnosis that the public is most likely to encounter — at the State Fair, in Las Vegas, on Television, or at a High School graduation — are for entertainment purposes and not what we do as professional hypnotists in the hypnosis office with our clients.

We don't ask our clients to cluck like chickens or bark like dogs.

We do help our clients eliminate the desire for smoking and drinking alcohol. We help our clients lose weight and eliminate years of painful experiences with an abusive partner or an abusive childhood.

The type of hypnosis that I teach (and that anyone willing to put time and effort into learning and mastering) is different. It's the type that you'll do in an office with clients who have debilitating fears, habits they want to be rid of, anxiety and stress that keep them from sleeping and excelling in life, as well as a host of other issues.

I remember it just like it was yesterday. I was in my office looking out the window. I had a number of meetings scheduled for the day. The work was interesting. The people I worked with were amazing. They were some of the smartest people in the world, and the work we did made a difference.

Yet, I still had this nagging feeling that in another twenty years, I would have spent the better part of my life sitting in this office, in front of a computer doing work that would be obsolete in three years. For all the good I was doing, it wasn't enough for me. I wanted more.

And then I went through a really low point. Devastatingly low. This book is not the one for that story. However, I did end up in a hospital contemplating whether I wanted to continue living any longer.

I knew something had to change, and that's when I found hypnosis.

It happened by accident. After the hospital incident, I began seeking something more meaningful in life. I had everything I was supposed to have – a great job, home, car, wonderful spouse, family, a 401k, vacation – all of it. But I wasn't truly happy. I began looking for something that brought meaning to life, something that was beyond the ordinary. I began seeking something more what people would call spiritual in nature – seeking meaning and true purpose in my life.

That's when I found hypnosis, and I understood what hypnosis really was.

I was reading a local paper advertising a course in hypnosis, and I took it. It was a good, entry level course. Yet I knew before it was over that it was not enough. When I completed it, I was curious and excited about hypnosis, but I didn't know what to do with my clients. I didn't know how to run a business; I didn't know how to bring in new clients. There was so much I didn't know. So, I looked for another course, one that would help me become a professional hypnotist. That's when I found 5-PATH® hypnosis, and after taking that course, that's when I was ready to see clients. Now, I understand the difference between just learning hypnosis and becoming a professional hypnotist, and that's what this book is all about.

Hypnosis allows us to reprogram how the automatic processes of our brain function at the root level. We can reprogram how we respond to situations and how we relate to people and circumstances. Hypnosis helps us to direct the functioning and abilities of the mind, including how the brain responds to sensory based information including our perception of pain. I had been programming computers for decades, and now I wanted to program the most powerful computing device available – the human mind. And I set out to do just that.

This book is not about my journey, but I will share parts of it to help you understand where you are at in your own journey and to understand if a career as a professional hypnotist is right for you and, if it is, if training in my program is the right choice or not.

Who This Book Is For

This book is for anyone who is considering becoming a professional hypnotist, for anyone who wants to help people in big ways — make life-transforming changes in the lives of others and truly help others with a heart connection.

This book is for life coaches, authors, massage therapists, counselors, and nurses who want a better way to bring relief and end the suffering of their clients. For healers of all types who want to learn the skills that hypnosis offers.

This book is for IT Professionals who have a love of computing and systems, who want to begin working with the most powerful computing device available — the human mind.

This book is for retired professionals and empty-nesters who want a dynamic and fulfilling career where they can set their own hours.

This book is for anyone with a servant's heart who wants a fulfilling and lucrative career helping people with the power of hypnosis.

How This Book Is Organized

You're reading the overview now, and I hope by this point you're interested in learning more about hypnosis, how it works, and how you can become a professional hypnotist. I've incorporated multiple levels of learning into this book – including client stories, hypnotic language, and metaphors to help you learn this material as quickly and deeply as possible. At some point, likely even before the end of the book, you'll know whether this is something you want to pursue professionally or not.

For now, here's a quick roadmap of what you can expect in upcoming chapters:

- Chapter 2 is The Truth About Hypnosis. What hypnosis really is and what it is not, the model of the mind, and different types of hypnotic inductions.
- Chapter 3 is Why a Systematic Approach is Necessary for Great Hypnosis Work. This sets the foundation for highly effective, modern hypnosis and advanced hypnosis techniques and why a systematic approach is vital for helping clients get repeatable results.
- Chapter 4 is Modern Hypnosis Techniques. The top ten crucial list of advanced and modern hypnosis techniques.
- Chapter 5 is The Hypnotist. Why the hypnotist using their own techniques and taking care of themselves is the most important element of amazing change work with our clients.
- Chapter 6 is Business Skills. The four most important business and hypnosis practice building techniques necessary to have a thriving hypnosis practice.
- Chapter 7 is The Mistakes New Hypnotists Make. Avoid these mistakes to save yourself time, and money, and hit the ground running with your new practice.
- Chapter 8 is The Next Steps. What next steps to take to get started on the path to your new career as a professional hypnotist now.

And the most important element, as you'll see throughout this book, is you – the hypnotist. This book is about you and for you.

I know what it feels like to feel lost and alone. I know how no matter how good you are at some things, if you haven't found your life's purpose or feel as if something is missing, then it's not enough. There's a yearning, a need for more.

The essence of life is growth. And we don't feel complete until we have become all that we can become.

If you feel that this is your calling, keep reading.

The Secret to Great Hypnosis Work

The secret is that every hypnotist needs to have a personal experience with hypnosis. The best hypnotists go into hypnosis while working with clients.

You may have already had a personal experience with hypnosis, and that's why you're interested in pursuing this profession. Or perhaps you had a loved one who experienced hypnosis. Or you're curious about how the heart and mind work and have looked at other related techniques such as flow state or meditation.

For my students, the personal experience with hypnosis is often related to overcoming a lack of confidence in business or hypnosis skills and mastery. You don't need any advanced skills now; you'll learn them. You simply need a big heart, desire to serve, and the courage to help people do things they've never been able to do – starting with yourself.

CHAPTER TWO

THE TRUTH ABOUT HYPNOSIS

"No matter what you think you are; you are always more."

– JOHN OVERDURF

I wrote this book to help compassionate humans understand how powerful hypnosis is and how rewarding it can be to do professionally.

I cannot take credit for all of the knowledge and information that I am sharing with you in this book. The ideas regarding how hypnosis works, how the mind works, and how emotions work, came from or were inspired by the work and teachings of Cal Banyan, my teacher. In this book, I add my own insights, tools, and examples to what Cal and other hypnotists teach as well, referenced in the acknowledgments section of this book.

Hypnosis Is Both Complex and Difficult to Define – and That's a Good Thing

If you ask ten hypnotists what hypnosis is, you'll likely get ten different answers. The truth is, there is no agreement on what hypnosis truly is.

And I am happy that we can't easily define hypnosis. Some of the most important and meaningful concepts in existence are difficult to define. Think about love; can you define love? What about beauty? Or grace? Or even a definition of God? Words can't properly describe these powerful concepts, and I think of hypnosis in the same way. It's complex and powerful, and defining it is difficult. Any words will fall short of the true essence of the power it offers.

And yet it's still helpful to attempt to define it. I'll begin with a current definition from Wikipedia, then a very brief history. This book is not intended to be a history of hypnosis; however, it makes sense to start at the beginning.

A DEFINITION OF HYPNOSIS

The definition of hypnosis, according to Wikipedia, is "a state of human consciousness involving focused attention and reduced peripheral awareness and an enhanced capacity to respond to suggestion. The term may also refer to an art, skill, or act of inducing hypnosis."

WHERE DID THE TERM "HYPNOSIS" COME FROM?

The word hypnosis was popularized by Scottish surgeon James Braid. The term comes from the Greek word *hypnos*, which means "sleep" because early practitioners believed hypnosis was a form of sleep.

We know hypnosis is *not* a form of sleep now, yet it is an altered state of consciousness – a normal and natural state of consciousness.

A MODERN DEFINITION OF HYPNOSIS

Here's my definition of hypnosis: Hypnosis is a state of mind where you are highly focused and receptive to positive suggestion.

In this state of mind, you become aware of things you weren't aware of before, leading to important insights and mental clarity.

These insights and clarity help you feel more secure and confident in everything you do and help align what you **want** with how you **feel** so you can more easily set and follow through on goals you have for your life.

Hypnosis is a Normal and Natural State of Mind, & Has Been Around as Long as Humans Have Existed

You've likely been in a state of hypnosis thousands of times in your life. It's as natural as being happy or intrigued.

Other terms that are associated with hypnosis include an athlete or musician being "in the zone" or when someone is in a state of "flow." They are both states of altered consciousness that can provide us with tremendous value.

COMMON AND EVERY DAY HYPNOSIS

Examples of common and everyday hypnosis include:

LOSING TRACK OF TIME

Losing track of time is an indicator of hypnosis. As a matter of fact, hypnotists will often use what's called a "time distortion convincer" to help clients realize they were in a state of hypnosis precisely because they underestimate their time in hypnosis.

When else do we lose track of time? Normally when we're doing something enjoyable like playing with our grandkids, or listening to music, or reading a great book. We'll get into why that happens in the next section on how the mind works.

WATCHING A MOVIE, LISTENING TO MUSIC, OR READING A BOOK

When you're watching a great movie, the storyline and characters captivate you. You become focused on the story and the setting the director has created for the scene. You are pulled into the characters, and you may even feel emotionally connected to the characters and feel sad when they feel sad or scared when they feel scared.

A great movie is captivating, and it's a common example of everyday hypnosis. If someone were to call to you when watching a great movie, you may not even hear them – you'd be so engrossed in the storyline.

The same isn't true for all movies though. Movies with difficult-to-follow storylines or poor lighting are hard to focus on. There are often too many distracting elements, and if the lighting, sound, or acting is poor, it's hard to get into the story.

The same is true for great music, concerts, and books. If they're good, we're captivated and pulled into the scene. We are fully present in that moment, a part of what the author, director, or musician is hoping for.

BEING IN NATURE

Being in nature is another common way that we go into hypnosis. Going on a beautiful hike and being captivated by the natural beauty of the landscape, getting away from the electronic distractors, and listening to the sounds of the forest, or the ocean, are ways we naturally go into hypnosis.

Have you ever had a great idea while out hiking in nature? That is the natural power of hypnosis at work.

BEING CREATIVE – PAINTING, SINGING, DANCING, POTTERY, WORKING WITH YOUR HANDS

This includes anytime you feel your creative juices flowing and that creating is easy. Ideas are coming, the words just flow, the artwork, pottery, keys, or strings are just dancing under your fingertips – that is a state of hypnosis. You are highly focused on one thing – whatever it is you are creating. You are accessing Life Force Energy! The energy that creates beautiful and wonderful things, that is what you are tapping into in that moment. And it's also a state of hypnosis.

Wouldn't it be nice to tap into that state on purpose, repeatedly and consistently?

That's what hypnosis offers: direct access to that heightened state of focus in order to do, be, and feel what we want.

HOW DO YOU KNOW THAT YOU'RE IN HYPNOSIS?

Hypnosis is not necessarily a feeling. And it's also not sleep. Hypnosis is focused awareness; focusing on some elements, while filtering out others. In the above examples, the environment or context is captivating. The scenery is beautiful and overwhelms your senses. While listening to music, or a movie, or reading a great book, the same is true – we're pulled in – immersed into the moment from their respective elements.

The focus that it naturally creates causes us to forget about things in our past and our future, and we become completely present in that moment. *That is what hypnosis is: the ability to focus and become completely present, with all attention on a single idea, element, or concept.* This is why we have a sense of losing track of time – because in hypnosis there often is no sense of time.

Hypnosis offers the ability to take all of your consciousness and focus it onto one coherent moment.

Would you like to have the ability to put one hundred percent of your brain power into a single moment, a single idea, a single effort? How powerful would that be?

A magnifying glass focused carefully on the sun's light can start a fire. Similarly with hypnosis, the focused consciousness it generates can help you fulfill your life's purpose and create the most breathtaking and amazing inventions, pieces of art or music, and moments in your entire life. It can help you overcome past issues, release painful experiences, and retain the lesson learned. It can help you become a fully self-actualized human being.

Hypnosis gives us the means to unlock the full potential of human consciousness.

Imagine – the full power of everything you truly are.

Without limiting beliefs of unworthiness.

Without fear of past failures.

Without negative past experience whatsoever.

Simply your true power as an eternal being focused into a single moment in order to fulfill your life purpose.

The Truth About Hypnosis

EVERYONE CAN BE HYPNOTIZED.

Anyone who is able and willing to follow instruction can be hypnotized, and people cannot be hypnotized against their will. It is a consensual state. It works best when clients really want to make changes in their life but are having a hard time doing so or a hard time following through.

HYPNOSIS IS NOT SLEEP, NOR IS IT RELAXATION.

This is a common misconception because we often have clients focus on relaxation in the hypnotic induction. However, hypnosis is not relaxation. Hypnosis clients are often in a state of excitement and bliss while in hypnosis.

HYPNOSIS CLIENTS ARE ALERT AND CONSCIOUS WHILE IN HYPNOSIS AND REMEMBER EVERYTHING SAID.

Many clients believe that while in hypnosis, they won't

remember anything that happened and that they somehow are unconscious or in an altered reality. The truth is that they'll remember it as much as they remember any conversation. Usually not verbatim, but they'll remember the summary of the session.

There are states of hypnosis that can be used for medical procedures; however, those deep states of hypnosis are not as useful in the hypnosis office as clients are not as responsive to the hypnotist, and doing great work with them can be difficult because the interaction is slow. For that reason, most hypnosis is done while in a conscious and interactive state.

HYPNOSIS IS NOT MIND CONTROL OR A TRUTH SERUM, AND HYPNOTISTS DON'T HAVE ANY CONTROL OVER CLIENTS.

The truth is that hypnosis is a consensual state. The hypnotist has no control over the client, and clients are not compelled to tell the truth while in a state of hypnosis. It's possible to lie while in hypnosis. Hypnosis is always an opt-in process with our clients. Hypnosis stage shows where people do incredible things is for entertainment, and that's not what happens in the hypnosis office.

How Does Hypnosis Actually Work?

In order to understand how hypnosis works, it's important to first understand how the mind works. Human beings are estimated to be around 200,000 years old. And our history and brain development are an important part of who we are and how we behave and think. The following is a model of the mind that helps to describe consciousness and the human experience to help you understand how hypnosis fits in.

THE CONSCIOUS MIND

The conscious mind is our point of focus. Whatever you are focusing on now, is where your conscious mind is. If you're reading or listening to this book, that is where your conscious mind is directed. If you're partially reading, while also day dreaming of being elsewhere, then your conscious mind is split between the two, and likely not doing a great job of either. If that's the case, you may need to re-read this paragraph to fully grasp its meaning.

Our conscious mind is analytical and rational. It craves certainty. It's where our logical thoughts and problem-solving mechanisms come from.

It's an important aspect of who we are and how we go about our day to day lives, do our jobs, interact with loved ones, and solve problems. It helps us set our schedules, create checklists and count change.

However, it's also limited. Scientists estimate that our conscious mind can only focus on seven to nine bits of information at one time. So, the conscious mind, although powerful, is not always the best part of our mind to creatively solve complex or challenging issues.

WILL POWER

Will power is part of the conscious mind. It is also energy driven, like a battery; when we're tired, our will-power is diminished. We must remember that we want to eat healthy, then follow through to use our will power. And if we're tired at the end of the day, we may not feel like eating healthy. We may choose instead to go out to eat and not have to hassle with cooking and cleaning, even though in the morning we were determined to stick with a healthy eating plan.

It's common to solve our problems with our conscious mind. Many hypnosis clients are highly intelligent and successful in multiple areas of their life. They can set goals and follow through. They critically consider what is working in their life and what is not and create an action plan to change.

That doesn't always work. Because our conscious mind is limited, it only has access to a small subset of who we really are. Anytime we're unable to use our routine methods to be successful, it's likely there is something deeper happening. It's as if there is missing information impacting our behavior. For that, we have to look to the bigger part of who we are – our subconscious mind.

THE SUBCONSCIOUS MIND

The subconscious mind is immense and unlimited. It's a memory bank of everything that has ever happened to you. It stores all of your memories, all of your emotions, and all of the meanings associated with all of the events in your life.

Your subconscious mind focuses on threats and opportunities and is expansive. It thinks in metaphor and symbols.

Your subconscious mind stores beliefs about yourself, both good and bad.

Your subconscious mind stores memories of past events, both good and bad.

Your subconscious mind stores habits that you use to go

about your daily life, both good (like brushing your teeth) and not so good (eating while watching TV).

And we are often acting upon information that resides in our subconscious mind without realizing it, because the information is not part of our conscious thinking.

So we feel bad, and don't know why.

And we do things we don't want to do, then get frustrated because we made a promise to ourselves about making better choices.

And what if there was a way to easily and purposefully access the information in the subconscious mind?

There is. And that is the power of hypnosis.

A GRANDMOTHER WITH A FEAR OF FLYING USES HYPNOSIS TO VISIT NEW GRANDSON [CASE STUDY]

Judy came to me because she was afraid to fly. She hadn't been on a plane in over twenty years. Now her daughter, who lived thousands of miles away in Florida, was having her first child, who was Judy's first grandchild. She wanted to be there for his birth.

In this case, Judy remembered when the fear began. She was on a flight that experienced significant turbulence. The plane shook and rattled, and there were a few tense moments. However, they were never in any real danger according to the pilot. It was a fearful experience, and she was grateful when the plane landed.

She hadn't flown since. Whenever she thinks of flying, her

heart races, and she can't think clearly.

And she knew what the problem was! She knew where her fear had originated but knowing isn't enough. It didn't resolve the issue. She tried other things first. She tried meditation and relaxing, but they weren't effective enough to get her on that plane.

Judy was able to fly again after three sessions of hypnosis. Hypnosis helped Judy rewire her brain to know that flying is safe and that she can fly to visit her grandson with ease. This rewiring is called neuroplasticity, and it's our brain's ability to change itself. Doing so for Judy meant she could fly with ease instead of anxiety.

She sent me a picture of her grandson weeks later, reporting that the flight was easy; she wasn't concerned at all. Instead, she was focused on her new grandson, just as we had discussed in her hypnosis sessions.

NEGATIVITY BIAS, JUDGEMENT, AND FEAR-BASED RESPONSE

An important part of our evolution is not only that we survived, but how humans survived. It's not that we're bigger or stronger than animals, because we're not. Some would argue it's because we're smarter, and that may be true. Others would say it's that we work together in social groups or tribes, and there's likely truth in that as well. One of the most compelling reasons we survived as a species though, is our ability to adapt to our environment. And the ability to adapt, is based on discernment.

Discernment is understanding what is important, and what is not. And our brain has developed, over thousands of years, to discern that anything that is life threatening is the most important thing to focus on.

Makes sense, doesn't it?

Scientists call this Negativity Bias, and it's a biological construct designed to help us focus on the negative for our survival.

If you've read any of my other books, then you're already familiar with negativity bias. It's an important concept because it clearly describes why our brain focuses on the negative elements of any experience.

Here's an overview of Negativity Bias, then how it plays out in our modern world:

WHAT IS NEGATIVITY BIAS?

Imagine that it's back in the Paleolithic (Caveman) Era, and you are running for your life. You are being chased by a saber tooth tiger (negative). As you're running, you notice a beautiful red apple (positive) – something you haven't seen in months. You'd love to stop and pick that apple, yet if you did, you'd likely be eaten by the tiger.

That negativity bias just saved your caveman or cavewoman life.

Our negativity bias has helped humans focus on the negative to survive, and it's a biological and natural response of our brain. Today it plays out in conference rooms and interactions socially.

Here's an example: You give a presentation on a topic that you have a lot of expertise on. The presentation goes well, and the audience is engaged and asking great questions. You answer all twenty of them – except one. One of the questions you're unable to answer. And it's not that you didn't prepare, it's that the question was out of scope of your talk. Yet it doesn't matter, does it? Because you want to have all the answers for your audience.

Later that day, when your loved one asks how your presentation went, will you mention the nineteen things that went well, or the one that didn't? *Negativity bias suggests you'll focus on the one thing you didn't do as well as you wished.*

And that negativity bias is the root of so much suffering.

We're afraid more than we should be. We have fear-based responses to things that aren't life-threatening. Being chased by a tiger is life-threatening. Being asked a question by comparison, is not. Yet the brain doesn't know the difference, because our perception of not knowing enough, or not being smart enough, equates to not being good enough. Not belonging. Not being wanted or desired.

And those feelings are rooted into the core of who we are, and self-worth. So, to our modern brain – *they feel life threatening.* And then we react accordingly, feeling bad, being too hard on ourselves. Not enjoying our life. And it plays out in real life as being nervous to talk in front of others, which in itself can make the talk less compelling.

We'll dive into how this issue can be resolved in later chapters, for now it's important to know that in order for us as humans to evolve and be our best – we have to Overcome our Biology.

And that is where hypnosis truly shines, because we can

overcome our biology and evolve with hypnosis and re-train the brain for excellence.

Human Consciousness Evolution Requires Overcoming our Biology

This section is about neuroscience. It's an important element for the modern hypnotist to understand how the brain functions. This material was influenced by the work of John Overdurf.

WE HAVE MULTIPLE BRAINS

What makes a brain? Neurons. And if neurons make a brain, then we have multiple brains.

And for the modern hypnotist, the most important element to understand is that the older, more primitive aspects of the brain **are still functioning along with the newer parts of the brain.**

And the newer parts of the brain were designed to over-ride the older circuitry. Yet that doesn't always happen. It takes focus and training to always operate from the newer parts of our brain, so here's a brief intro:

1.   REPTILIAN BRAIN

The oldest part of our brain. It knows two things: fear and pleasure.

This is where our primitive fear-based responses come from, like freeze, fight, and flight.

The pleasure that we are born with includes: food, thirst, and reproduction. It's important for us to develop pleasures from other elements in our life – like art, reading, music, connections, and nature. Otherwise if we don't have those developed, the reptilian brain will revert back to one of the primary pleasures. Weight gain, and bad habits can be the result.

2.   THE MAMMALIAN BRAIN

Is where more complex emotions arise. This is where our limbic system resides which includes the amygdala, hippocampus, and the hypothalamus. This is the seat of our judgements that we make, which are often unconscious and often related to our survival – is this person or event a threat to my survival?

3.   PRE-FRONTAL CORTEX OR NEOCORTEX

This is the newest part of the brain that scientists call the "executive function." This is where language was developed, and our desire to work together socially was developed as well. Abstract thought and imagination are also part of this aspect of the brain.

Hypnosis and Brain Coherence

Brain coherence is the measure of how effective different parts of the brain communicate with each other. A highly coherent brain is like a well-designed transportation system where cars (nerve impulses or synaptic transmission) move easily along super highways (neuropathways) and there are very few traffic jams or detours (clarity of thought and creative thinking). A highly coherent brain is correlated with intelligence, learning ability, creativity, performance, and emotional regulation and maturity.

Mindfulness techniques such as hypnosis and meditation can increase brain coherence over time. I believe in a state of hypnosis the brain can actively become more coherent – which is one reason that clients have "a-ha" moments in hypnosis. The brain has made a connection between previously disparate parts which provide clients with massive insight during the hypnosis session. These moments of insight can provide life-changing behavioral and emotional shifts that have been difficult for clients to achieve up to that point.

Why Does Any of This Matter to Hypnosis?

As hypnotists, we want to understand the human condition. We need a strong foundation for what is happening in the hearts and minds of our clients in order to truly help our clients.

The truth of the human condition is that we are often responding to our surroundings from our reptilian or mammalian brain. We feel fearful, or judgmental, yet we don't know why because the underlying reason is not conscious to us. This is very frustrating to feel things, or do things, and not understand where it's coming from. We can feel out of control. This common and protective response to situations is often referred to as a part of the brain called the critical factor. The critical factor serves as a gate-keeper for the subconscious mind, and it's an important part of hypnosis to help our clients override the critical factor to positively interact with the subconscious mind. More details on this in forthcoming chapters.

PERCEPTION AND RESPONSE IS HOW IT ALL FITS IN WITH HYPNOSIS

We really only have two things in life that we can control, one is what we pay attention to, and the second is how we respond.

The first, what we pay attention to, is about our perception.

We may perceive something as being dangerous, and our heart may start racing. There may be a news program on the television, and as you watch it, you notice your heart begins racing. And you can also turn the television off, and not pay attention to it. So, our perceptions and control of our attention is important. We always have control over what we pay attention to, yet it often takes discipline and practice to follow through on what we want.

Second, we can control how we respond to situations that may be out of our control. And for this scenario, it's likely that we feel compelled to pay attention because of the nature of the situation itself. Someone is hurting us or someone we love, and we don't want to shift our attention. Instead, we can shift our response.

WHAT DOES THIS HAVE TO DO WITH HYPNOSIS AND NEUROSCIENCE?

Knowing how the brain is designed to *focus* on threats and *filter out everything else* is an important step in overcoming the limits of the critical factor.

Hypnosis is a focusing technique to quiet the fear anger and other negative emotions that our lower functioning brain is designed to latch on to. It puts us in the driver's seat of our best thinking, and increases brain coherence to facilitate potential life-changing moments of insight.

Hypnosis helps us gain a deeper understanding and mastery

over our attention, perceptions, and responses.

HYPNOSIS IS LIGHTING QUICK – JUST LIKE THE BRAIN

The brain can retrain itself and learn important concepts in near-instantaneous time, and hypnosis allows us to optimize this ability even more. It provides the environment for the brain to learn lightning quick by focusing everything on a particular moment to gain important insight.

Take for example something many people seek relief from through hypnosis: phobias. A phobia is considered an "irrational fear" of something. An irrational fear of driving may keep someone at home instead of using a car to get to the store for medicine or food.

Driving is inherently dangerous. People die and are seriously injured in car accidents all the time. In 2017, there were 31,000 vehicular fatalities. But a phobia of driving, also called vehophobia is when the fear is irrational. It would be someone remaining at home and not getting food or medicine they needed because of a fear of driving. Phobias are a medical term and are diagnosed by a medical practitioner.

The brain learns fear in a millisecond for survival, including phobias.

It can also release that fear if it's erroneous, in a millisecond.

The brain can learn to be afraid of spiders in a millisecond, called *arachnophobia*.

And it can re-learn to instead be *cautious* around spiders in the same amount of time.

For many clients, they're effectively driving around in an old beater car with a flat tire. Because they're allowing their fear-based primitive brains to be in charge of their conscious thinking.

And with hypnosis, we're giving them the keys to a Ferrari — fast, responsive, and very powerful. It will take them wherever they desire to go.

We all have access to the best parts of our mind when we begin operating from the newer circuitry. Hypnosis helps us do that on purpose.

How Does Modern Hypnosis Help our Clients?

Most clients come to a hypnotist as a last resort. Hopefully that will change and as hypnosis and the modern techniques that are repeatable and get massive results for our clients grows, more people will turn to hypnosis initially for help, instead of as a last resort. Most hypnosis clients have tried other things to help them, including counselling, coaching, dieting, 12-step programs, self-help books, spirituality, religion, and support groups. And each of those techniques can be helpful. Yet if it's not solving the problem for our clients, then hypnosis is an excellent solution for one primary reason:

Hypnosis, *when done well and using the right techniques and procedures*, works by tapping into the subconscious mind and releasing unresourceful and limiting beliefs, habits, and emotions. In contrast, most other techniques focus on cognitive or conscious thinking, and they can provide results. When they don't, we must go deeper.

Here's why modern hypnosis works so well:

1. HYPNOSIS REVEALS THE *REAL* CAUSE OF THE ISSUE – NOT WHAT WE *THINK* THE ISSUE IS

With hypnosis, we get information from the subconscious mind. This is information that is usually *known* to the client, but not known to be impacting them.

For example, a client may *know* they were bullied as a child. What they may not realize, is that the feelings and beliefs that were created as part of that experience are still having a major impact on their behavior. Many clients will report, "I knew that happened, but I worked on it already, and thought it was fixed."

Without hypnosis, we're often working on the wrong issue! Or believe the wrong issue is the cause of our problems. Hypnosis offers clarity on complex issues and situations.

2. HYPNOSIS HELPS ALIGN WHAT WE KNOW WITH HOW WE *FEEL*

We almost always do what we feel like. It's rare for us to do something we don't feel like doing, unless we're highly disciplined. And even then, we do it for the end result of *feeling* or *being* a certain way.

Hypnosis helps us to feel how we want in the moment, so it's easier to follow through on important behavioral choices. Imagine, what if you always *felt* like eating healthy? What if you always *felt* like being active? Would it be easier to stay healthy if you always felt like doing the things that are indicative of a healthy human? Of course it would! We just don't always feel like it, do we? We get tired, the cake or cookies sound good. We don't feel like going on the walk.

Hypnosis works in that feeling space, so we get to align how we feel (I feel like eating healthy), with what we want (I want a healthy body).

This happens because we "light up" (or activate) the part of our brain that is associated with those thoughts and feelings by focusing on them. As that part of the brain becomes activated, the associated thoughts, feelings, and behaviors can be changed on purpose with hypnosis. This ability for our brain to change is called neuroplasticity.

This helps clients feel *unstuck, and also allows them to follow through on recommended actions from their coaches, mentors, and medical providers.*

3. HYPNOSIS GIVES US CONTROL BACK

With hypnosis, we get control back. We get to operate from the newer parts of our brain, and eliminate those old, useless and worn out limiting beliefs and erroneous emotions. We override our fear-based responses to things, and start operating from the evolutionary newer part of us. The smarter part of us to lead a more fulfilling life where we feel in control. We know what we want, and we feel like doing it, so we follow through. We feel in control.

4. CLIENTS GET UNSTUCK AND OUT OF NON-RESOURCEFUL STATES

Often clients come to us because the existing tools they're using aren't working, and they feel stuck. They're stuck in unresourceful states. What I mean by that is a state of mind that is not helpful for them.

This is usually because what they have been using has been from their conscious thinking alone, which as a reminder is very limited. Again, the power of hypnosis comes from the ability to tap into the subconscious mind. From there we can uproot the limiting beliefs, old fear-based emotions, and eliminate them to get our clients unstuck and moving again.

5. HYPNOSIS HELPS TO BYPASS CONSCIOUS RESISTANCE TO CHANGE

Conscious resistance, or as some people call it the critical factor, is that part of our mind that is at all times trying to protect us. It rejects anything we don't already believe to be true.

Have you ever met someone who just can't take a compliment? No matter how truthful, or genuine your compliment is, they just can't allow themselves to believe that you are being honest with them?

And the reason for that, is what we call limiting beliefs. For that individual, they were likely belittled, or bullied, or not cared for properly at some point in their life. They learned to believe that they are unworthy of love or affection, or compliments. And no matter how much you see the beauty in them, they can't see it for themselves.

Helping this type of person, or client, can be difficult if you're only using conscious-based tools. Because the critical factor, or conscious resistance, will protect this person and not allow any of your genuine compliments to be believed. They'll smile and say thank you, but they won't really believe you, it won't sink into their heart.

With hypnosis, we bypass that critical factor, and go directly to the subconscious. There is still a part of that human who knows she is lovable, who believes she is good, and worthy, and who will accept your compliments. And as a hypnotist, she will accept and allow you to help her release those old limiting beliefs, and negative emotions associated with them. Even if they're decades old.

6.   HYPNOSIS ELIMINATES ERRONEOUS BELIEFS AND NEGATIVE EMOTIONS

Hypnosis powerfully helps to eliminate past limiting beliefs and negative emotions stored in the subconscious mind. You may be surprised to learn how easy this is to do with clients. The reality is that we are often behaving based on experiences stored in the subconscious mind, but we rarely consider how to make changes to the information (beliefs and habits), and feelings (emotions) stored there. Hypnosis gives us direct access to make changes to that vast, unlimited part of ourselves.

ISSUES MODERN HYPNOSIS HELPS WITH

Hypnosis is known for helping people eliminate fears and phobias, lose weight and stop smoking. Yet it can also be used for all sorts of other behavioral issues, such as nail biting, hair pulling, stopping drinking, increasing motivation, and being more active.

It's also used to help resolve past issues, like negative childhood experiences where people felt unloved, and unworthy.

Those issues often show up in their current lives as adults, as having difficult relationships with their parents, siblings, and even spouses and coworkers, and as behavioral issues as well with food, drugs, and alcohol.

Hypnosis can help reduce the sensation of pain in the body and help clients who are faced with debilitating diagnoses and illness, such as cancer and end of life issues. Medical issues are always conducted with a referral from a medical provider, and hypnotists often work in conjunction with a client's medical team. Hypnosis can also reduce the suffering associated with injury and illness. It can help clients with the loss of livelihood, of dignity, and grief.

Hypnosis can be used to help people excel as well and be their best self. To become excellent at everything they do and enter a highly focused and productive state of mind repeatedly, on purpose.

It can help improve public speaking, increase motivation, help entrepreneurs and business leaders crystallize ideas and communicate more effectively to grow their companies. It helps business owners get over money blocks, and rapidly grow their business by helping gain clarity on vision and goals.

Hypnosis done well can be used for any issue because it's about helping us be our best by focusing our entire consciousness on the present moment. The here and now. Not past fears. Not limiting beliefs.

So, when clients ask me, can hypnosis help me with (fill in the blank)? The answer is always a yes!

In the upcoming chapters, we'll dive into how modern hypnosis techniques are designed to work in a systematic way, and how the old style of hypnosis is replaced with newer, modern techniques that get our clients repeatable results.

Make sure to download the complimentary tools that go with this book, including the *Can You Be a Hypnotist?* Checklist, and the free online masterclass *Can You Be a Hypnotist?* Both are available at **http://CanYouBeaHypnotist.com/.**

The next chapter is all about the need to have a systematic approach to hypnosis – a model, that will help us help our clients in an expected, repeatable way.

CHAPTER THREE

A SYSTEMATIC APPROACH TO HYPNOSIS

"Ruthless Compassion. Be willing to do the difficult work with your clients, powerfully and with great compassion."

– CAL BANYAN

A systematic approach to hypnosis is the key to getting repeatable results with your clients, and there are many good reasons for this that we will go over as part of this chapter. The primary reason listed below however is the most important:

A systematic approach to hypnosis works because it allows you to be fully present with your client.

You won't be worrying about what script to use; you won't be shuffling paperwork, wondering if your client is at the right depth of hypnosis, or scrambling for a technique.

Instead you will be connecting with your client. You will know they are at the proper depth of hypnosis for the deep work you want to do, and fully engaged in solving their issue with great hypnosis work.

Elements of a Hypnosis Session

Before we dive into the new, modern style of hypnosis, it's important to have a foundation for what a typical hypnosis session is like. Here are the components that will be referred to in this book.

1. Hypnosis Patter
    Patter simply means *prepared words* in a hypnosis suggestion or script. "Relaxing more and more with every gentle breath you exhale" is hypnosis patter.

2. Hypnosis Pre-talk
    A conversation with clients where we help them understand what hypnosis really is and eliminate common myths about hypnosis. The second chapter of this book on hypnosis could be considered a hypnosis pre-talk, in written form, yet it's more in-depth for readers who are considering becoming professional hypnotists. This is usually done only once with each client.

    One of our primary jobs as hypnotists, is to help our clients remove resistance to change, and be willing to get rid of the elements that caused them issue to begin with.

    The hypnosis pre-talk helps to eliminate resistance to change, and resistance to doing hypnosis.

3. Pre-Hypnosis Interview
    A conversation with clients prior to every hypnosis session where we discuss their desired outcomes, results for the week, and anything else pertinent to our work together. This happens every session.

4. Hypnosis Induction

A technique including hypnosis patter where clients enter into a state of hypnosis. Not all hypnosis inductions are created equal, and it's important to have at least one hypnosis induction that works in minutes and brings your clients to the desired level of hypnotic depth. However, you also do not need dozens of hypnotic inductions either. A few highly effective inductions are preferred for the professional hypnotist.

5. Testing and Convincing

A professional hypnotist will test clients for hypnotic depth, and once that is complete, will use specific hypnotic phenomena to convince clients that they are in hypnosis. This will deepen their hypnotic state.

6. Hypnosis Insight Work

Insight work is done while in a deep state of hypnosis to bring clients relief. Insight work includes: Age Regression and Progression, Forgiveness Work, Parts Mediation Work, as well as other powerful perspective shifting techniques that brings our client instantaneous and lasting relief.

7. Direct Suggestion

Direct suggestion, or hypnotic suggestion, is what most people think of when they think of hypnosis. A direct hypnosis suggestion is directly suggesting something to your clients that will help them achieve their desired result. For example, a direct suggestion for someone wanting to lose weight would be "You only eat when you are actually hungry, and the pounds melt away easier than ever before," and for someone wanting to increase their confidence "You think more clearly, speak more easily, and feel confident in your ability to do whatever it is you want to do in your life with grace and ease."

Direct suggestions are important and powerful, and they are still a part of modern hypnosis – however they have a tendency to fade if not reinforced. The preferred method is to use both insight-based techniques, along with Direct Suggestion for lasting benefit.

8. Emerging from Hypnosis
   Emerging the client includes using hypnosis patter to guide the client from a state of hypnosis back to their normal level of consciousness.

9. Post-Hypnosis Interview
   A conversation after the hypnosis session to reinforce insight gained during the hypnosis process and answer any questions from the client.

Classic Approaches to Hypnosis

I am grateful for the classic approaches to hypnosis, because they have brought us the modern techniques we use today. This book is not going to cover all of the "old" ways that hypnotists used to work. You're welcome to review all of that on your own, if you wish. Instead, this chapter will review some of the common classic techniques in comparison to the modern techniques, and why they are important.

CLASSIC APPROACH: PROGRESSIVE RELAXATION HYPNOSIS INDUCTION

You are likely familiar with this common style of hypnosis induction. Here's an example of the patter: "And now bring your attention to your feet and as you do, your feet easily and effortlessly release all tension, and you sink further into a deep state of relaxation."

It is very relaxing, and comforting, and it's also slow. It can take up to twenty minutes. It also does not bring clients to a specific depth of hypnosis. It is a useful hypnotic induction to induce sleep, and that's exactly how I use it for my clients who are having problems sleeping. I don't use it in the hypnosis office, however. We don't want our clients going to sleep during session. We want them to get the results they came in for.

MODERN APPROACH: INSTANT AND RAPID INDUCTIONS

The modern approach to hypnosis inductions include rapid and instant inductions, including affect-based inductions and confusion-based inductions.

A rapid induction, like the 5-PATH Rapid Induction, or an instant induction, uses specific techniques to help our clients enter into the state of hypnosis in a few moments, or minutes.

An affect-based induction uses the clients current emotional state as a hypnotic induction.

A confusion-based induction focuses the conscious mind and occupies it fully with contradictory or ambiguous language to allow direct access to the subconscious.

These inductions are preferred because they help our clients enter into a state of hypnosis in a few minutes. They include tests and convincers to ensure our clients are at the proper depth of hypnosis for us to do the deep and advanced insight-based work we want to do with them to get them rapid results. The next chapter includes further explanation of some of these inductions.

CLASSIC APPROACH: READ A HYPNOSIS SCRIPT

This could be a script the hypnotist wrote specifically for that client or modified from another hypnotists' script. Most hypnosis scripts will include elements to engage the client's imagination, and also direct suggestion.

Either way, this style of hypnosis is primarily one-way – the hypnotist is doing all or most of the talking, and the client is listening. There is nothing wrong with this style of hypnosis - some clients will find it very comforting and relaxing – perhaps like a relaxing massage for the mind. However, it is not as powerful or life-changing as insight work. It's difficult to achieve results for our clients without interactive communication – how will you know what impact the hypnosis is having on your client without it?

This is also the style of hypnosis that you will find online, and as downloadable hypnosis recordings.

Part of the design of this style of hypnosis is the client is expected to listen to a recording of the session daily. And it works as long as the client continues to listen regularly. If they stop listening to the recording, the suggestions and impact fade.

MODERN APPROACH: INSIGHT-BASED TECHNIQUES LIKE AGE REGRESSION, FORGIVENESS WORK, AND PARTS MEDIATION WORK, THEN FINISH WITH DIRECT SUGGESTION

Insight based techniques are the modern and more powerful approach to use with clients. They include Age Regression, Forgiveness Work, Parts Mediation, and other perspective shifting techniques that do one important thing for our clients:

Insight Based Hypnosis Techniques help create a-ha moments for our clients that change their life... in an instant.

Have you ever had a moment of insight? An a-ha moment, where everything clicked and made sense – and it seemed to happen all of a sudden? These a-ha moments occur in the hypnosis office nearly every day when we're using the right insight-based techniques with our clients.

The reason this happens, is because while in a state of hypnosis our brain becomes more coherent. Different parts of our brain that have not been connected before, are connecting while in a state of hypnosis and using the right insight techniques. This brain coherence facilitates a-ha moments for our clients and offers life-changing results.

How Systematic Approaches Work to Bring Relief to Clients

Systematic approaches to hypnosis work because they allow you to be fully present with your client and you won't be taking time searching for a script that may or may not suit your client's needs.

But what does a systematic approach look like, and how do they actually work?

Systematic approaches to hypnosis are designed with the following key elements in mind:

1. Results Oriented: Clarity of Outcome and Measurable Results
    A systematic approach to hypnosis means we are focused on *results* for our clients.

    It's a common mistake for new hypnotists to make to want to focus on telling potential clients all about the hypnosis, and hypnosis techniques they are using. And in reality - most of our clients don't care about the hypnosis. Not really. *They want results.* They've tried everything else. They're tired, and close to hopeless. They're not entirely hopeless or they wouldn't be reaching out for help at all.

    They want to lose weight, they want to sleep better, they want to stop drinking or smoking, they want to feel more confident at work. And while it can be important to help our clients understand why hypnosis can work when other techniques have not, the real way to help our clients is to get them the results they came in for.

    We do that by establishing a very clear set of benefits and outcomes from the beginning with our clients to ensure we're working on the right issue, and we'll know for certain when the results have been achieved.

2. Criteria Based
    Every step of the hypnosis session has checkpoints along the way to make sure the hypnotist knows when to move on to the next step. No guessing.

3. Incremental and Ongoing Success and Feedback from Clients
    We get ongoing feedback from our clients and with measurable results, we know what is working, and what needs further refinement.

4. Follows a Normal and Natural Flow of the Human Experience and Emotional Pathway
A systematic approach follows a natural pathway of human emotional experiences.

Most of our clients come to us because they've been unsuccessful using their normal methods of change. For example, some people will try reading a book, support groups, goal setting, an app, or will power. When their standard methods fail, they may turn to hypnosis.

At the root of their inability to do what they want, is almost always some level of fear.

Even 50-year-old high-level and successful executives and CEO's that I've worked with have fear. There is still a scared little boy or girl inside that desperately wants to be loved and cared for, who wants to feel worthy, feel safe, and know that someone truly loves them.

Fear is what we will help our clients be rid of. And to do that, we start with hope.

The systematic approach I use and teach is called 5-PATH. 5-PATH stands for 5 Phase Advanced Transformational Hypnosis. It was developed by my teacher and mentor Cal Banyan. This book is not exclusively a 5-PATH book, yet the underlying principles of 5-PATH are an important element to powerful and lasting hypnosis, and they are described here for reference.

5-PATH CONSISTS OF FIVE PHASES:

Phase I of 5-PATH is about brining hope to our clients and

ensuring they are open and prepared for hypnosis work.

Phase II of 5-PATH is about eliminating erroneous beliefs (limiting beliefs), and emotions, including fear.

Once we eliminate erroneous beliefs and emotions, there is often anger associated with those negative situations. We resolve useless and unnecessary anger next.

Phase III of 5-PATH is about eliminating useless and outdated anger at others.

After our clients are feeling more peaceful and happy, and the fear and anger are gone, there's often feelings of guilt. Our clients wish they would have made changes earlier or are upset at themselves for the things they did or did not do, for not being kinder and more compassionate to themselves, or not treating themselves with the respect, dignity, and love that they offer others in their life.

Phase IV of 5-PATH is about eliminating useless and outdated anger and guilt towards themselves.

Most of our clients are feeling fantastic at this point. Many have carried around negative feelings of low-self-worth, fear, anger, and guilt for decades! And they've buried it under decades of eating too much, or drinking too much, or physical pain, or not living their life to its fullest. By discounting themselves and living in shame and remorse.

Some of our clients will have what's called secondary gain. Secondary gain is a secondary reason to hang on to their pain.

Phase V of 5-PATH is about eliminating secondary gain.

Here's an example of secondary gain: Imagine Grandma Betty broke her hip. She's recovering at home, and since she's not supposed to move, her grandson Bobby visits her a few days every week to bring her groceries, mow her lawn, and visit with her.

It's been a few months, and Grandma Betty's doctor is happy with her progress – but Grandma Betty still reports significant pain. The doctor is surprised, as there's nothing to indicate Grandma Betty should still be in pain.

In this case, Grandma Betty is hanging onto her problem – her injured hip, for a secondary reason. If she gets better, her grandson won't need to visit any longer.

This secondary reason for Grandma Betty to hang onto her pain is what we call secondary gain. The primary issue (the original break), is healed. It's the secondary reason that Grandma Betty is still having issues. To resolve this for Grandma Betty, her grandson could offer to visit regularly, or she could find other ways to spend time with people.

Another example is with Laurie.

Laurie came to me to lose weight. She had tried everything to lose weight in the past, and she was able to lose the weight, yet it always came back.

With hypnosis and the Reprogram Your Weight system of weight loss that we use at our center, Laurie was losing a few pounds every week, and she was happy. She started dancing again and felt energized when she woke in the morning and excited to start her day.

On her fifth session of hypnosis though, she reported feeling a little down. She hadn't lost weight that week, as a matter of fact she went out with her friends on Thursday night for happy hour and ate too much. She ate like she used to eat – without thinking about it, and she also had an extra glass of wine.

She felt terrible, and wondered if hypnosis was going to turn out the same way as everything else she had tried.

And instead, what we discovered in hypnosis would have a positive lasting impact on Laurie's life- and her husband's life.

In a deep state of hypnosis called somnambulism, Laurie realized that her husband was feeling a bit jealous. He didn't like all the attention his wife was getting, and she was going out more frequently than she used to, and he missed her. Laurie hadn't realized this consciously – she didn't connect the dots. Yet in a state of hypnosis it became clear to her why she chose to over eat on Thursday.

Feeling relieved, she returned home and made some changes with her husband. They went away for the weekend together. She focused on him, and they spent quality time together. She shared with him what transpired, and he felt terrible that he gave her that impression. They grew closer. And they decided to start being healthier – together. He joined her on her morning walks. They cooked together. Through this experience, they grew closer, and got healthier.

Laurie connected with me a few months later and reported that her weight loss had continued – and he husband had lost ten pounds as well! They were happier than ever.

I hope you enjoyed this introduction to modern hypnosis and why a systematic approach is so important. Without knowing about secondary gain, some hypnotists can miss the signs for helping clients who struggle with secondary issues. Instead, they may work on the wrong problem with their client, and clients won't get as good or as rapid results. Having a systematic approach with clients helps us to get great results for our clients, consistently.

In the next chapter, we'll dive into the top insight-based techniques for the modern hypnotist.

CHAPTER FOUR
MODERN HYPNOSIS TECHNIQUES

Julie came to me to lose weight. She arrived five minutes late and a bit frazzled – she couldn't sit still in the chair.

A few minutes into the initial consultation however, we discovered that the *real* issue was alcohol. She said, "I always start planning to have two glasses of wine, and it always ends up being the whole bottle."

Her first session was emotional and insightful. She arrived with her paperwork in hand, sat down at my desk, and we reviewed her goals. She wanted to stop drinking to feel better. To lose weight. To increase her confidence and have a better relationship with her husband.

I asked her, "What would your life be like if you this wasn't an issue for you anymore?"

"I'd be much happier, and not worried that my husband was going to leave me. Or that my kids would be disappointed in me," she said.

Alcohol was ruining her life, she reported. She already quit her job – before I got fired, she said. Her kids didn't trust her anymore, and her husband wasn't happy with her. Her life was chaotic and frustrating.

"I started drinking when I was fourteen. It was the first time in my life I wasn't nervous."

And in that first session she couldn't sit still either.

She fidgeted around in the chair as we went through the Hypnosis Pre-talk, and she had the common questions about hypnosis – including *is hypnosis mind-control*, and *will I remember anything?* At the end of the Hypnosis Pre-talk, she was feeling better, so we moved to the hypnosis chair to begin the hypnosis portion of the session.

In that first session of hypnosis, she had a remarkable realization.

After testing for hypnotic depth, and even further hypnotic deepening, I used a technique with her called Age Regression. I wanted her to experience good feelings, and asked her to feel peace in her body, and then go to a time where she felt the most peaceful in her life. Then I helped her focus on feeling good – without alcohol. And she had some powerful insights about what her body and mind *really* wanted from the alcohol. "I thought I was drinking to calm my nerves. And I realize now, when I drink too much, it actually makes me feel nervous. I have to find another way."

After emerging her from hypnosis, she looked different.

Calm. Peaceful. With a moment of clarity, she turned to me and said "Erika, I forgot what it felt like to feel at peace. I haven't felt that good in decades."

Seven weeks later, she arrived for her final hypnosis session. She had over six weeks of sobriety behind her – along with a new life. She was happy. The frazzled woman who arrived late to my office had been replaced by a carefree, relaxed, and confident version of herself. She was radiant. There was a calm assuredness about her that was comforting. "Erika, I have my life back. I have my husband back, and I realize the alcohol was just keeping me stuck in a terrible dark place. I've also lost a few pounds. Thank you for giving me my life back."

Julie's story of triumph is common. And it's always such a joy, and I have deep gratitude for helping people in such tremendous ways. There is so much suffering in the world that can be alleviated with a few sessions of high-quality hypnosis. And after working with thousands of clients on a variety of issues, there are techniques that I've found especially valuable.

This chapter includes ten of the most effective modern techniques for the professional hypnotist. These are the techniques I use in my office day in, and day out, and what you'll notice is that not all of them are specifically hypnosis. Hypnosis is, after all tapping into our subconscious mind and getting more information. Getting information is not enough – it's what we do with the information that is beneficial. And what we do with the information inside and outside a state of hypnosis is extremely valuable, for our clients will leave the hypnosis office and we want them to get results when they leave our office.

#1: The Setup

The most important part of a hypnosis session – is not actually hypnosis. It's in what's called *the setup*. The setup is everything you do to prepare your client for hypnosis. And when done well – the hypnosis is easy.

Here are the components of the setup:

1. Connecting to the most important client
   Who is your most important client? The one in front of you. Professional hypnotists will see two to six clients daily. Prior to the next client arriving, it's important to clear your mind of anything unrelated to that client. I have a focused routine I go through for each client, where I clear my mind, enter into a state of hypnosis (see *Going into hypnosis first*), and prepare to focus everything that I am, on that client.

2. Going into hypnosis first
   Professional hypnotists do their best work while in a state of hypnosis. They focus only on the client in front of them and getting that client the result they desire. The hypnotist goes into a hypnotic state first – and our clients more easily enter into hypnosis as well.

   This is because not only will a professional hypnotist use a highly effective hypnosis induction with their client but knowing that as humans we learn more by showing (being in hypnosis first), than telling (speaking), our clients more easily know what we're asking them to do, and follow suit.

Confidence

The number one reason clients don't go into hypnosis is fear. Professional hypnotists build confidence in three things in the hypnosis session:

• **Confidence in the hypnotist:** the hypnotists' reputation and communication – including website, images, online presence and appearances, and written material.

• **Confidence in hypnosis:** An effective hypnosis pre-talk that eliminates fears about hypnosis and helps our clients know what hypnosis actually is – a safe, normal, and natural state of mind they've already been in thousands of times.

• **Confidence in themselves:** Once our clients have confidence in us as a hypnotist, then feel confidence in hypnosis, we want them to have confidence in themselves, and that they can get what they came in for.

3. Clarity of Results and Outcomes

Clients don't come to a hypnotist for hypnosis – they come for results. And getting them their desired result begins by clarifying what they actually want, and how will they know when they get it. Here are the elements of clear results:

• **Focus: One issue at a time:** Client issues are complex and multi-faceted. They'll report multiple issues – for example a client will report an issue with their boss and eating too much and gaining weight, which also keeps her up at night so she's also not sleeping well. However, attempting to resolve sleep, stress, weight gain, and an issue with the boss all at the same time, will get her minimal results in all areas. The desired approach is to clarify which of these elements, once resolved, will have the largest positive impact – and resolve it first.

• **Measurable results:** Being "happier", or "more peaceful", is nice. However, it's hard to measure. And when our clients don't *know* that they're getting better, they may think the hypnosis isn't working, and worse yet that there's something wrong with *them*. On the other hand, when we ask for clarification, for example, how will you know when you're more peaceful? And get a measurable result, for example "I'll fall asleep within fifteen minutes every night," now our clients know they're getting better, which increases confidence in themselves, and their work with the hypnotist.

• **What they *do* want:** Many clients have been stuck in a negative state for so long, that they really don't know what they do want, and will only report what they don't. For example, clients will report "I don't want to feel so stressed", "I don't want to feel so out of control", and it's important to clarify with them – what they actually do want instead. For example, you'll ask "If you weren't so stressed, how would you feel?". It may take some clients time to find an answer – they've been stuck in fear and anxiety for too many years to consider something other than fear and anxiety. *For some clients, this is the most critical shift you can help them make initially – helping them to think about what they actually do want.* Consider this – if they've only ever been focusing on not wanting to be stressed or anxious, what do you think that creates in their mind?

Try it now:

Read the following two sentences, and notice how they make you feel, and what you think about:

I don't want to be so stressed an anxious all the time.

I feel peaceful and calm, and there's an element

of comfort and serenity with me wherever I go.

Which of those two feels better to you? Hopefully your answer is the second, because it's actually stating what is wanted, not what is unwanted.

#2: *Rapid and Instant Inductions*

Classic forms of hypnotic inductions could take twenty minutes or more, and they do not include hypnotic depth testing.

Professional hypnotists use modern inductions that are:
- **Fast:** modern inductions help get our clients into hypnosis in a few moments – as in the case of an instant induction, or minutes.
- **Criteria based:** modern inductions include checkpoints along the way to ensure our clients are at a specific level of hypnosis depth.
- **Include depth testing:** modern inductions test for hypnotic depth to ensure our clients are at the proper depth of hypnosis before we begin.

Dispelling myths about hypnosis inductions:

Myth: You need dozens of hypnosis inductions for a variety of client personalities and issues.

Truth: You only need a handful of highly effective inductions.

Myth: You should use a different induction every time with clients, or they'll get bored.

Truth: Clients appreciate the same induction every time – it becomes familiar to the mind.

Truth: Use the hypnotic induction that is best for your clients at the time – if they are presenting with an emotion – use the Affect Based Induction. If they present with an old, outdated pattern, use a pattern-interrupt induction.

Myth: You should deliver your hypnotic induction in a slow, deep voice.

Truth: Deliver hypnotic inductions with a fast cadence using your natural voice. Speaking too slowly allows the client's conscious mind to interfere with the hypnosis process. The best hypnotic voice to use is your own natural voice. It does not need to be a deep voice. And if you try to simulate a deep voice, it will not sound natural, or congruent and it will sound "off" to your clients which will interfere with the hypnosis process. Congruency of tone is important for delivery of hypnosis. Your voice and tone should be congruent with what you are suggesting. Having a deep, monotone voice will likely be boring and put your clients to sleep.

The four hypnotic inductions every hypnotist should have mastered include:

- **Instant Induction:** an induction that works in seconds.
- **Rapid Induction:** an induction that works in minutes.
- **Affect-Based Induction:** an induction that utilizes our client's present emotional state.
- **Confusion, or Pattern Interrupt Induction:** An induction that interrupts our client's pattern or causes confusion in the conscious mind which offers direct access to the subconscious mind.

#3: Emotionally Driven Techniques and State Elicitation

We almost always do what we feel like. Think of the last time you had to do something you really didn't feel like – a common thought is "fine I'll do it, but I don't feel like it!" So, wouldn't it be great to always feel like doing what you want to do?

What would happen if the smoker never felt like smoking? Or the drinker didn't feel like drinking?

An advanced and powerful technique to help our clients eliminate a bad habit is to get to the feeling they have right before they decide to do what they don't want to do and eliminate it. It works for positive emotions as well, get to the feeling that they have right before they do something courageous, and successful – and repeat it!

WHAT DOES STATE ELICITATION MEAN?

State elicitation means to help our clients experience a state of being, or state of mind. For example, happiness is a state. Confidence is a state. Hypnosis helps our clients to elicit certain positive states of being on purpose, like confidence when public speaking, and peace when there's chaos all around. And also eliminate unresourceful states, for example recognizing a stressful state of being, and using hypnosis techniques to transition to a wanted state – for example peace or focus.

#4: Incremental Success

Incremental success is a powerful tool that helps our clients recognize their own success – even the small wins. It is the opposite of negativity bias because it focuses clients on what is working, instead of the few things that are not, as in Michelle's story below.

MICHELLE REVISITS THE PIZZA MONSTER [CASE STUDY]

Michelle was visibly upset when she came in for her second session of hypnosis. "I ate pizza again" she reported, her voice full of disappointment.

"OK, we'll get to that in a moment, first tell me, what *did* work for you this week?"

She pondered the question for a moment. "Well, I only had two pieces of pizza, not four. And not the rest the next day either, so I guess it was a lot better than normal."

And this is common for clients. Because of negativity bias, they'll report the negative first, and an advanced and important technique is to use incremental success to point them at what worked instead.
"Great, so are you saying you ate twenty-five percent of the pizza you used to eat? Do you think that will help you?" I asked.

"Yes," Michelle replied.

"And what would happen if you ate no pizza, at all, would that work?"

"Maybe, but I've done that before, and it doesn't last," replied Michelle, a bit of hope returning to her voice as she realized how a healthy balance is more important than the all-or-nothing approach.

IMMEDIATE GRATIFICATION AND DELAYED DISCOUNTING

Our brains want to feel better *now*, and a big part of what we help our clients with is overcoming the desire for immediate gratification in exchange for long-term results. We will offer our clients alternatives for immediate gratification – including incremental success, instead, so they can have both immediate gratification (I ate only two pieces of pizza, and lost one pound this week), and long-term results (in two months she'll be down ten pounds).

Delayed discounting is a term that explains how our brains will discount any benefit that is delayed. And weight loss is a prime example. The brain wants the cookies now, not waiting for weight loss two months in the future! And understanding that the brain discounts perceived future benefits helps professional hypnotists to bring the concept of immediate gratification in the form of incremental success to our clients, so they can experience gratification *now*.

For Michelle, it went like this:

"Michelle, I want you to realize something. You ate twenty-five percent of the amount of pizza you used to eat. It was not only do-able, but it was easy. You still enjoyed your pizza, you didn't feel bad about eating it, and you lost weight. This is the balance that is so important for you. So, let me ask you one more question – do you think you can do this – eat like this, for the rest of your life?"

"Yes, I think so. It's easier than trying to not have any pizza at all. And it's definitely better than eating the whole thing."

"Good. This is a healthy balance for you. You did well. It's not an all-or-nothing approach that will work. You get to feel good *now*, because you got to enjoy your pizza, *and* lose weight! How does that make you feel?"

"So good!" she replied, now beaming with the realization of her new approach. That is the power of incremental success paired with an understanding of negativity bias, delayed discounting, and how to actually meet the needs of the brain.

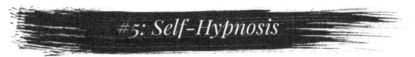

#5: Self-Hypnosis

Self-hypnosis empowers our clients to use hypnosis on their own, in between sessions and for the rest of their lives to be successful.

Everything we help our clients to achieve while working with them, should be reinforced in self-hypnosis practice, and I highly recommend teaching your clients self-hypnosis while working with them.

There are many forms of self-hypnosis. The most powerful one for your client will be the one they actually use. It should be easy to do anywhere, easy to remember, and provide results in a short amount of time. Simplicity is the key. The form of self-hypnosis I love to use with clients is called 7th-Path Self-Hypnosis and it was developed by Cal Banyan.

Many clients have success with meditation, and others struggle with meditation. We don't want to add to our client's frustration or lack of confidence.

MEDITATION AND SELF-HYPNOSIS

There is an overlap between meditation and self-hypnosis.

Both produce a peaceful and focused state of mind. The difference is that hypnosis is focused on an outcome that is correlated with the hypnotic suggestion. If the hypnosis suggestion is to feel relaxed, then relaxed is the desired outcome. If the hypnosis suggestion is to eat only when hungry, that is the intention. Meditation is powerful and focused on clearing the mind to experience our true nature beyond normal thought.

Both are powerful states, both are important. Self-hypnosis can be easier, since the intention can be single-purposed and simple. The simplicity allows our clients to get relief and feel successful.

ARE YOU GOING ON A RUN, OR A WALK?

I've completed sixteen marathons. They all took significant and focused training.

And now, on any regular week, I may leave the house at seven in the morning and walk, *meandering*, wherever I feel like for a few hours. I can head towards the water, or downtown. I can cut through a park or neighborhood.

The meandering style of walking is what I would compare to meditation. It's pleasant and peaceful.

However, when I'm training for a marathon, meandering won't do. Under those circumstances while training, instead I'll leave the house and purposefully complete a ten-mile run to a very specific destination. I will time it and bring water and food.

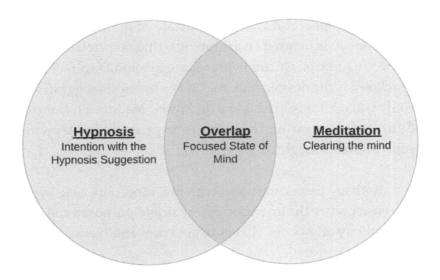

Training for a marathon is more purposeful. It's intentional. Meandering every weekend wouldn't be enough to prepare me for a marathon.

So, *meandering is like meditation, and intentionally running a set distance is like hypnosis.* They have similarities, but hypnosis will get you where you want to go faster.

#6: Neuroscience

Neuroscience is the study and understanding of the structure of our nervous system and the brain. Understanding modern neuroscience helps the professional hypnotist understand the experience of our clients and what the brain is doing.

WHAT IS THE PURPOSE OF THE NERVOUS SYSTEM?

The goals of the nervous system are to:
1. Collect sensory data from the body and outside world
2. Process and interpret the data
3. Respond appropriately to the data

Understanding how our nervous system works, helps us understand why our clients respond to situations in certain ways.

THE FLOW OF PERCEPTION*

The flow of perception explains how our sensory data plus our internal belief systems and habits help shape our experience.

$$X > M > F > B > R/Tr$$

X: Something happens, and we perceive it from our senses.

M: Meaning is applied. This meaning comes from conscious mind. We call them thoughts. The meaning also comes from our subconscious mind, and we may not be consciously aware of this information. This means we can react and behave based on information we're not consciously aware of. Some people call this intuition, it's a knowing or feeling beyond rational thought. The meaning applied to any situation is often incorrect or includes limiting beliefs that hurt our clients.

F: Feelings are generated in the body which provide a feedback loop. For example, we feel fear in the body in a particular way, and when we do, we can take appropriate action on it.

R: Reaction, often one we don't want including an over-reaction.

Adapted Flow of Perception by Cal Banyan

Tr: Thoughtful Response, an intentional, thoughtful response. A Thoughtful Response is what we're always aiming toward, and good news: over time a Thoughtful Response can become a reaction.

A WALK AROUND THE PARKING LOT

Mike works at a car dealership as a customer service representative. He processes customer orders for service being done on their cars.
And his boss is always stressed.

Today, like most days, Mike's boss yelled at him because the coffee machine in the customer waiting area was messy. Someone had spilled coffee, and it hadn't been cleaned up. A customer complained about the disarray.

Why didn't I realize this happened in the break room? Mike thought. And he felt worthless. If the customer would have only come to me, or I would have checked in there earlier, I could have avoided getting yelled at.

And before he realized it, Mike was in the break room getting a candy bar from the vending machine, again, even though he planned on eating healthy today. *I guess today isn't the day to start eating healthier – I'll try again tomorrow, he thought.*

X: Something happens > Mike's boss yells at him.
M: Meaning is applied > I'm worthless. I should be able to do a better job.
F: Feelings are generated > Mike feels worthless.
R: Reaction > Mike gets a candy bar from the break room to feel better.

NOW WITH HYPNOSIS

Same scenario, yet this time Mike has been through a few sessions of hypnosis to reduce feelings of stress and worthlessness.

This time, when Mike's boss yells at him, Mike realizes that the break room gets messy – and it's impossible for him to do his job while checking in on the break room every minute of the day. It's his boss that actually has the problem, and so he doesn't let his boss's behavior negatively impact him.

Instead, he goes on a walk around the building to de-stress.

X: Something happens > Mike's boss yells at him.

M: Meaning is applied > John (Mike's boss) is really stressed, and often takes it out on me. I know he's really stressed with his own issues with his son at home, I feel bad for him.

F: Feelings are generated > Mike feels sorry for John, yet also realises his behaviour is unprofessional.

R: Reaction > Mike takes a quick walk around the parking lot and is inspired to find work that he truly loves.

Hebb's Law and Neuroplasticity

Hebb's law is the following "Whatever *fires* together *wires* together". Developed by Dr. Donald Hebb, Hebb's Law explains that in the brain, if two neurons fire together, they wire together. This is the basic building block of a habit.

If you eat while watching Television, the neuropathways that fire when eating, *will be physically located in the brain in proximity to or directly connected to the ones for watching television.* This is why people who are accustomed to watching Television while eating will have a hard time watching Television without eating – because those two actions (eating and watching TV) are wired together in the brain.

Thankfully, neuroplasticity is brain's ability to re-wire itself. And that is what we help clients do every day in the hypnosis office.

The Fifteen Second Rule

Brain scientists used to think the nervous system could generate a feeling for ninety seconds. The feeling is designed as a feedback loop to get our attention – so we can become aware of something that we have perceived and take action.

For example, *Fear* is designed to tell us there is something potentially dangerous happening, and to flee or take precaution.

And now, brain scientists tell us the nervous system generates feelings for fifteen seconds.

Fifteen seconds.

A craving will last, at most, fifteen seconds.

Unless we focus on it. Then the fifteen seconds starts all over again.

TRY IT FOR YOURSELF WITH ATTENTION SHIFTING AND

PATTERN INTERRUPTION

Next time you have a craving, or a painful thought – something negative you don't want to be feeling, doing, or thinking about, put your attention on something else. This is called attention shifting or thought stopping. And the way it works is you must first become aware of the thought or behavior and interrupt it.

Interrupting an existing pattern is called a Pattern Interrupt. Think of it as a detour on a neuropathway – you want to interrupt that existing pattern (thought, feeling, or behavior), and redirect it elsewhere. Next, choose *ahead of time what you're going to think or do instead*. Otherwise, it won't work.

Why do we have to choose a better thought or action ahead of time?

Professional Hypnotist Truth #1: When we are in a low energy state we do not have access to our higher thinking.

A low-energy state just means we are experiencing a low point in the day. We may be physically, emotionally, mentally, or spiritually tired. In that state we don't think as clearly or expansively as we would like to.

Write down what you want to think about or do instead, for example how much you love your kids, or your pets, or your spouse. Or think about the time you had that amazing experience. Or plan on going on a short walk or listening to a favorite song. Write it down now.

Here's the good thought or action I'm going to take the next time I want to practice Attention Shifting:

Now, next time you have a craving, or a thought you don't want to have, the first step is to become aware of it. We can't make any changes without awareness. Here's the process:

1. **Pattern Interrupt:** this is awareness of the thought or feeling you don't want to have and stopping it (the detour).
2. **Attention Shifting:** purposefully shift your attention to a better thought or activity that you've already selected.
3. **Notice in fifteen seconds (or sooner) the thought or feeling will be gone.**

The only reason it seems like the thought continues longer than fifteen seconds is that we continue focusing on it, so it's regenerated by the nervous system.

The Label Maker of All That Is Good and Bad

Our conscious mind is so good at pattern matching, and it loves to categorize, generalize and label things. Experiences and situations are "good" or "bad" in general.

And for many people, that's the extent of their emotional labelling.

Fear is different than anger. And sadness is different than fear.

However, for many people, *those* feelings are simply "bad."

It is critical that clients become aware of their actual feelings and use more descriptive terms other than just "good" or "bad," otherwise they feel stuck.

JASON SETS HIMSELF FREE FROM BAD FEELINGS

Jason came to see me to stop drinking. He walked off the job days prior for being upset at his new boss – someone with no experience in his field at all.

He walked out, drove straight to the liquor store, and bought a pint of whisky and a six pack of beer.

He knew he was in trouble and was worried he would get fired or get into more serious trouble if he didn't control his anger.

And he was angry. That's what he was aware of. And yet throughout our sessions together, something else became apparent.

He wasn't just angry. He was sad. He was grieving the loss of his wife and his brother.

Yet the only feeling he was aware of or would talk about was the anger. And felt like he was "stuck" in that feeling.

I asked, "How are you feeling?"

"Bad," was always his answer. And if I let him off with that limited response, we may not have found out what was really happening.

"Use a more descriptive term," I pressed.

He paused... I waited.

Tears started pouring, slowly from the corners of his eyes.

"I miss John so much. I miss Emily." He was talking about his brother and his wife.

I didn't let Jason get away with a response from the conscious mind that was not true. Maybe feeling "bad" about his new boss was easier for his heart to handle, but under the surface, he was still grieving the loss of his brother and wife. Once we addressed those issues, he didn't feel stuck anymore, and he also wasn't angry at his new boss. That was irrelevant to him now.

Jason went back to work later that week and talked with his boss, and they worked things out. His boss admitted he didn't know what he was doing. This was a new role for him, and he appreciated Jason's support and insight. Jason realized he didn't want to be the boss either!

Uncomfortable silence and pauses reveal truth.

Professional Hypnotist Truth #3: Our conscious mind does not like uncomfortable pauses or silence. It wants certainty. Be patient with clients, allow the pause to reveal the issue. The response will likely be a true gem from the subconscious mind.

He liked his role working with his hands; he didn't want to manage people. It was a win-win. And Jason stopped drinking, and instead went back to working out at the gym regularly. He was at peace with his brother and wife's passing, and began living a life he enjoyed with friends.

#7: Age Regression

Age regression is the most powerful technique we have as hypnotists because it is the way the brain is designed – to remember important aspects of past experiences in order to make decisions in the present moment or the future. It happens normally and naturally every day.

Age regression in the hypnosis office is where we purposefully ask our clients to return to a particular state of mind, or point in time, in order to gather insight into the *meaning that was created from that situation, so it can be changed if desired.*

The purpose of age regression is not to have clients re-experience events, it's to have them *shift the meaning that was applied based on those events. The original meaning is often painful - I'm not good enough, or I'm a bad person.* And the original meaning is often coming from limiting beliefs and feelings generated from other people in the experience who were also hurting (parents or siblings), or from a lack of experience or maturity (being a child).

The reason it works is that the brain doesn't distinguish any difference between a real or imagined event – so an event that is remembered with the imagination, can bring up the same feelings as the original experience.

TRY IT FOR YOURSELF

What's your favorite song from high school or junior high?

The one that still gives you chills or good feelings? Take a moment and think of it now. Once you have the song and are feeling how it used to make you feel, continue reading below.

Now that you have the song, I want you to re-experience the song in a situation when you heard it so long ago. For example, you may be in your car with friends, at a concert, or a dance, or maybe in your room listening on the radio, cd, or tape recorder.

Imagine it as-if that experience is happening all over again. Feel what you were feeling, let it be as if you are *really there*.

That is age regression. Our brains can revivify – re-experience something that happened years ago. And it's happening to hypnosis clients without them realizing it all the time. They'll feel worthless from a "look" a stranger gives them because it reminds them of how their father used to look at them. Or, they'll feel bad when they perceive that colleagues are gossiping about them – as in the case of Cindy below.

CINDY MAKES PEACE WITH MS. BILLOWS [CASE STUDY]

Cindy came to me to lose weight. She ate healthy at breakfast and dinner, which is surprising since most clients have their biggest eating issues with dinner and after dinner snacking. But with Cindy, her biggest issue was snacking at work.

And, like many clients, she *knew* what her issue was, but that wasn't enough. Knowing her problem was not enough to help her stop it. There was much more going on.

Cindy described to me the last time she snacked at work, which happened to be the day prior. I asked her to go back *right before she started snacking* to tell me how she was feeling. We always go right *before* the behavior- not during the behavior. We want to know the thoughts and feelings prior to making the decision to snack.

The technique is called a Date-time Age Regression, because I'm asking her to go to a specific time, based on an event. There are other types of Age regression too, for example an Affect based Age Regression, Symptom Age Regression, and Cognitive Age Regression.

I asked Cindy what was happening, what she was thinking, and how she was feeling in that moment before she decided to snack and eat something she knew she didn't want to eat.

"I'm anxious. My co-worker Amy just looked at me and whispered to my other co-worker Michelle. I know they're bad talking about me."

I asked her about the anxiety, and she said she always has that feeling before snacking, so I asked her to follow that feeling to an earlier time in her life when she felt anxious just like that.

"I'm in school in front of the classroom, in second grade. It's Ms. Billows' class. It's show and tell. I'm holding up a picture that I drew of my neighbor's horse, Lacey."

"She telling me it's the worst horse she's ever seen in her life, and now the entire class bursts into laughter. I want to die."

"Cindy," I ask, "What do you wish you would have known back then about this situation, and about Ms. Billows, that you know now?"

After a few moments of thought, Cindy continued. "I wish I knew that Ms. Billows just lost her baby. I didn't know that then. I learned that years later."

"I know it wasn't me or my horse, she was just hurting in her own way."

That insight healed decades of pain for Cindy, for she was right. Ms. Billows never should have acted that way. Yet the reality is grown-ups act improperly all the time because they too, are hurting.

Hurt people, hurt people.

Professional Hypnotist Truth #3: People who are hurting inside often behave inappropriately, and in ways they later regret and often hurt others in the process. It doesn't make sense to continue to suffer from their hurtful behaviour, we can understand that hurt people do hurtful things, and rise above that situation to experience a more peaceful and enlightened existence.

When Cindy saw her coworkers whispering about her, it wasn't just that instance that her nervous system was responding to. It was responding to all the times in Cindy's life where she was made fun of, picked on, and bullied – including with Ms. Billows. This is why we can feel so out of control. Our subconscious mind tries to protect us from these old, outdated feelings, but under the surface, we're still feeling them. They're still impacting us.

Even something that happened years ago still impacts our behavior until it's resolved.

Time does *not* heal old wounds.

Professional Hypnotist Truth #4: Time does not heal old wounds. The wounds - physical or emotional, must be healed by specific healing techniques - usually inherent to our own bodies. Time is simply passing. Take a cut finger for example, time is not healing a cut finger. Your body is healing it. And you can block that process by not taking good care of your cut! The same is true about emotional healing. And that is learning how to avoid the same situaiton in future. Our brain is primarily focused on keeping up safe, so anything that hurt us in the past, it'll remember until the lesson is learned and can be avoided in the future.

JOAN IS STILL UPSET WITH HER MOM [CASE STUDY]

Joan called me and asked if I could help her with something she's been struggling with for over eighty years. She was *still* mad at her mom for embarrassing her when she was five years old. It stung back then, and it still hurt – eighty years later. Joan was eighty-five.

In hypnosis, Joan was able to forgive her mother, but it was so much more than that. Because, as usual, Joan *knew* what she wanted to do, and *knew* what needed to happen. She knew she needed to forgive her mother, and she had tried but the feeling remained. *Knowing* is not enough. Do you find that frustrating? I did until I realized what was actually happening.

Knowing what to do isn't always enough. Sometimes we need to *feel* it too.

Professional Hypnotist Truth #5: It can be frustrating but knowing isn't always enough to fix issues in our lives. Sometimes it is. We often solve issues merely by researching and 'figuring out' what to do. And that is using our conscious mind to solve the problem. If that isn't enough, then it's often that we know we should do something, but we don't feel like doing it. And for that, we need to employ the subconscious mind to help us resolve that issue. And tapping in to the subconscious mind is easy with hypnosis.

In a state of deep hypnosis called somnambulism, Joan realized why her mother embarrassed her. It came from her mother's own fears and insecurities. She didn't like what happened to her, but she understood it and was able to forgive her mother.

She released the old feeling of anger by *transforming* it to gratitude and peace for her mother.

We don't really let go of feelings. We transform them. We change them. Joan transformed her feelings of fear and anger (embarrassment for her) to gratitude and peace for her mother. The anger was gone, and she had a new understanding based on love and grace.

We don't release old feelings; we transform them in to better feelings.

Professional Hypnotist Truth #6: We don't discard or get rid of old feelings. Not really. We transform them. This is an important

> *truth about the nature of the human experience. Consider a painful experience from your past. You're not leaving it along the roadside of your past, discarded and unwanted. Rather you are inspecting it, looking closely at what it has to teach you about yourself and your life. Once understood, it is transformed automatically to something beautiful. A lesson learned, adversity overcome, a painful experience transformed to a beautiful expression of wisdom and compassion.*

#8: Shifting Perspectives

Have you ever wished you could step outside of yourself, and gain a fresh perspective on a situation, or life in general? With hypnosis, it's not only possible – it's a very powerful and purposeful technique.

JIM FINALLY APPRECIATES HIS STRICT UPBRINGING [CASE STUDY]

Jim came to see me to improve his public speaking. He was the CEO of his corporation, and the company was growing and expanding into new markets around the globe. He regularly spoke to his small team of about ten and annually to his entire team of thousands. He wanted to ignite passion and drive into his employees.

And he was also a self-describe perfectionist. He reported always being that way based on a strict-upbringing by his military father.

In a deep state of hypnosis, I asked Jim to imagine being

his father. Imagine what it was like to have a son like *him(self)*, and what that would be like?

"I feel the heaviness of my father's struggle. He grew up so poor. His own father worked so hard, yet they never had enough. His father didn't finish school. They survived many months by scourging for food in the woods and forest during the depression. It's so heavy, and painful."

After releasing tears and decades of generational pain, Jim continued, "My father never meant to be so hard on me. He only wanted me to avoid the pain and struggle he endured, and saw his own father suffer with. My grandfather felt like a failure, because he couldn't properly provide for his family. Even though so many others were suffering in the same way, at the same time. My father vowed to not let that happen to us. That's why he was so strict. That's why nothing less than perfect was allowed."

And for Jim's father as a young child during the depression – anything less than perfect could mean starvation and possibly death.

Not only did Jim improve his public speaking, he also realized something so vital about himself, and the human experience. We all have long-standing and deep-seated fears that are impacting us. We have generational stories that are part of our own story, that if we don't address can negatively impact our lives.

Jim took his experience of being his father, and it helped him to understand what his customers may be feeling. He used the same technique to understand what his employees may be feeling. The things they are afraid of, the things that keep them up at night.

And it changed him; it *empowered* him.

More information offers us choice and the power to freely choose is liberating.

Professional Hypnotist Truth #7: Hypnosis does not fix our clients. It offers them more information - we call it insight. And with insight, we have more choice. The power to choose what we want to do. The power of choice is liberating. We are no longer stuck in knee-jerk reactionary behaviour. We can choose how we want to respond.

#9: Honoring Different Parts of Ourselves with Competing Desires

We all have different parts of ourselves that have different goals. For example, there's a part of you that may want to wake up early in the morning and go on a run. There may also be a part of you that instead wants to stay in bed and have another cup of coffee or tea.

Both of these parts are valid, and at times one may win out over the other. This is normal and natural, and we all experience it. You'll hear it in everyday language as well, "I don't know, a part of me wants to go to the party, but a part of me also wants to stay home and just watch a movie."

It's a normal experience for humans to have competing desires. They arise out of our longing for different things:
• We want to interact socially *and* have fun and to relax at home

with a movie
- We want to be healthy *and* feel good and to relax in bed with loved ones
- We want to have a successful career *and* to spend quality time with our family

And our clients will experience the same things while working with us:
- They want to lose weight *and* still go to the party
- They want to stop drinking *and* stay in contact with their best friends
- They want to stop smoking *and* feel peaceful

And a great way to help our clients do this is with a technique called *Parts Mediation Work*.

Parts therapy has historical roots in family therapy, and is often credited to Richard Schwatrz, a family therapist, who developed parts after listening to his patients describe different parts of themselves, they were struggling with. It was Cal Banyan who first developed Parts Mediation Work as a non-hypnotic process that was conducted as a psychological process used when two individuals were in conflict. Then when he entered into the profession of hypnotism, he created Parts Mediation Work™ as we know it today, where the hypnotized client is divided into two parts, the part that wants to change and the part that wants to continue in the old way (or any other internal conflict). This approach is used to resolve secondary gain issues that can cause a client's issue to continue after the causal work has been completed. It resolves that conflict and provides insight so that the client can experience long-term change.

Do Hypnotists have *clients* or *patients*?

Hypnotists have *clients*.

Medical and Mental Health professionals have *patients*.

It's an important and clear distinction to make as we do *not* want to give our clients the idea that hypnosis is medical in nature. It is not. And for many of my clients, they are happy it is not medical in nature, as they have not been happy with the results from Westernized medicine. Hypnotists can work on medical issues with a referral from and in congruence with the client's medical provider. This is how we can help clients with pain.

The goal of helping our clients with parts mediation, is to meet the common goals of both (or all) parts of the client, by revealing the underlying reasons for the desired behaviors as in Barb's Story below.

BARB'S NIGHT OUT [CASE STUDY]

Barb was doing great losing weight. She had lost almost ten pounds in the month she had been coming into hypnosis, and more importantly, was enjoying her life again.

So, I was surprised when she came in reporting she gained weight this past week.

In hypnosis, Barb had the insight that she was hurt by a comment her husband made about her weight loss. He felt left out. She was spending more time with friends and at the gym then she was with him. He wasn't happy with the change, although he was happy to see her happy and healthy.

Barb didn't want to hurt her husband, and yet she realized she had changed:

- She didn't enjoy sitting in front of the television any longer. She wanted to be out going things.
- She didn't want to go out to breakfast, she wanted to be out walking or kayaking.
- She didn't want to go to the movies, instead she'd rather see a live show, or get to bed early so she could be out at six a.m. for a ride.

And her husband was getting left out. All of those old ways of doing things were things they did together.

- He didn't join her on her early morning runs.
- He didn't go with her kayaking.
- He didn't go out and listen to live music.

His feelings were valid, and she loved him.

In hypnosis and using Parts Mediation, Barb devised her own plan to satisfy both parts of her – the part that wanted to lose weight, *and* the part that loved and wanted to spend time with her husband.

Instead of a more sedentary activity like a movie, or television with her husband, she asked if they could go do something more active. They bought a local hiking book and started checking off hikes together one by one. Being in nature and having the high quality alone time is exactly what her husband needed, and also fit perfectly into her new lifestyle.

PRAISE THE PROBLEM TO UNDERSTAND THE BENEFIT

Help clients by praising the problem and understand how it is serving them. Asking questions such as, "how is eating too much serving you?" may seem like an odd question, but it can help set clients at ease, and will provide insightful answers.

For example, a client who reports eating too much may state if they're overweight, then they won't be hurt again by a partner as they had been in the past. The real issue is helping the client heal from this past relationship, and over-eating is the symptom. And the food itself provides comfort. So, the approach would be to heal the past relationship issue and provide the client with a new form of comfort.

Many hypnotists make the mistake of vilifying our client's issues, which naturally creates resistance. Every problem our client has is serving them in some way – even if it's minor or seems illogical.

#10: Hypnotic Language and Suggestion

A hypnotic suggestion is a powerful method of programming your mind for things that you want.

Your subconscious mind is always listening in on your internal thoughts, and that is why it is so important to watch your internal dialogue and get rid of any negative self-talk that comes from our negativity bias.

Positive language and thoughts can be empowering.

And the hypnotic suggestion is an important tool for hypnotists to use with clients. We want to directly suggest to our clients, in plain language, what we want them to do.

And we want to do it indirectly as well. Both techniques work. Both are valid.

The most powerful hypnotic suggestions come from our clients, and a great hypnotist will listen carefully to their client's language and write down the important aspects of what they communicate. It's common for clients to say what they actually want out of hypnosis during the first session. For example, a client may report "I just want to be fully present and connected with my audience when I'm speaking." Then, during the hypnosis session they'll realize an insight such as "I've always been good enough, it was my mother who couldn't love me out of her own insecurities."

That type of insight can heal decades of low self-esteem. Then, by directly suggesting – or repeating back to our clients what they came in for, we can help them get their desired result. For example, "and now that you know you've always been good enough, it's easy for you to be fully present and stay connected with your audience."

The above technique is called The Segue to Direct Suggestion. It's connecting the dots between the insight work in the hypnosis session (I've always been good enough), to the direct suggestion they came in for (thinking about things other than food, and losing weight).

Our subconscious mind responds best to simple, direct language.

Our subconscious mind loves metaphor, and symbols.

Storytelling will be a great tool for you as a hypnotist, to help your clients with powerful hypnotic suggestion.

The most hypnotic words are the ones that you will use in session with clients every day to help your clients.

A SHORT LIST OF THE MOST POWERFUL HYPNOTIC WORDS

1. *Wonder, Curious*
    Saying "I wonder" or "I'm curious" to your clients automatically initiates a subconscious response.
2. *Imagine*
    Asking our clients to imagine something also automatically initiates a subconscious response.
3. *Because*
    Because is a very powerful word. It's sneaky in its simplicity and everyday use. Because offers a reason to the subconscious mind for the statement to be true. It makes the statement reasonable, logical, and attractive to the subconscious mind.
4. *You [Your Name]*
    You, and the more personal version, your actual name is very hypnotic. It's been said there is no sweeter sound, than the sound of your own name. When we hear our name, we are captivated.
5. *The More*
    The More you read this material the more you are curious about hypnosis and the power of the mind. The More is a powerful hypnotic word that allows the hypnotist to build one phrase on top of another. This is similar to As.
6. *As*
    As you listen to my voice, it's easy to focus your attention inward

and relax even more. This is similar to The More.

7. *Pretend, or Just Pretend*

Pretend is a hypnotic word, it is initiating the subconscious mind. Pretend that you are going more deeply relaxed and notice how good that feels. Pretend works because it takes the pressure off of the client to do things perfectly right. Just pretend you're doing it right, and they'll likely start doing it right.

PUTTING IT ALL TOGETHER

Putting together a combination of these ten techniques, along with a systematic approach, covered in chapter 3, makes for a very powerful system of hypnosis.

Yet, the hypnosis is not the only ingredient to being a successful hypnotist. If you really want to have a thriving practice and change lives, you also have to take care of yourself, and know how to avoid common entrepreneurial and business pit falls, which are covered in the next two chapters.

CHAPTER FIVE
THE HYPNOTIST

"Enlightenment is always preceded by confusion."
– MILTON H. ERICKSON

There is a secret to exceptional hypnosis work with clients.

It isn't the most effective techniques. Those techniques *are required, and very important* – yet they can be learned by anyone who puts time and energy into their craft. This is *not* a secret.

It isn't marketing either. Again, those skills can be learned, and you can hire experts with skills to help you grow your business. This also, is *not* a secret.

It's not the latest technology to reach your clients or streamline your business. Those can be helpful, but they're also *not* a secret.

The secret to great hypnosis work, *is in you - the hypnotist.*

This is what I call *Personal Alignment,* and it is the secret to exceptional hypnosis work.

Personal Alignment is your relationship to yourself and the world. It's self-care and wellness. It's your ability to show up as your absolute best, knowing you will learn and get better every day. And the most amazing aspect of this is that you have 100 percent control over it. No one can ever take it from you. It's yours. Forever. You have 100 percent responsibility, and you have 100 percent control.

Most hypnotists don't want to focus on themselves, they want to focus on the practice and their clients.

And I want you to know that the energy you bring to your practice has everything to do with your success.

- Not just the techniques, tools, or systems
- Not just the marketing or networking
- Not just the business strategies
- It's within you – the hypnotist, and how you show up every day.
- Feeling overwhelmed with too much to do can cause a sense of scarcity and fear
- Feeling nervous to talk about what you do will limit the clients you reach
- Feeling a lack of confidence in talking with clients will keep them from wanting to sign up and work with you
- Feeling as-if you have to have all the latest techniques will keep your head spinning, instead of centering your heart on what brings value to your clients

I have one task. One goal, one thing I am constantly doing in my business. I'm asking myself: *How do I get even better results for my clients and grads?*

And I know for certain that if I am feeling expansive, focused, and operating at 100 percent, I will deliver exceptional results to my clients, and grads *every single time.*

So, what are the keys to personal alignment?

It's really good hypnosis – on yourself!

The Keys to Personal Alignment

There are 5 keys to Personal Alignment that will help you be an exceptional hypnotist:

1. Be a true believer in hypnosis
2. Recognize that any perceived issue in your practice must be resolved in you first, before it will be resolved in your practice
3. Do your own work, daily
4. Connection with yourself first is required
5. Love is always the answer

1. BE A TRUE BELIEVER IN HYPNOSIS

It's imperative that hypnotists are true believers in hypnosis. This means you have had a personal experience with hypnosis that lets you know beyond a shadow of a doubt that hypnosis is real, and that it works wonders.

Hypnosis Magic

Hypnosis is *magic*. Because it offers us solutions that we don't quite understand yet. Over time, you'll be able to look back with hindsight and realize – it wasn't *really magic*. It just seemed so at the time. Magic is just something we don't quite yet understand.

I want you to have seemingly magical experiences in hypnosis. This is how my courses are designed, for you to have a personal experience in hypnosis – maybe magical, that shifts how you think and feel. That proves to you that hypnosis *reveals the issue*, even if it's something you've been struggling with for a long time. And after revealing the issue, it shifts how you think and feel about that issue, and you feel better. You're able to shift behavior, and your automatic response is thoughtful, happy, and peaceful. You're no longer overwhelmed with negative thoughts or anxiety.

Experiencing the transformative power of hypnosis on a personal level is so vital to becoming an exceptional hypnotist that it warrants its own Professional Hypnotist Truths, shared throughout this chapter.

> *Professional Hypnotist Truth #8: Hypnosis is different, and you can expect different results.*

When you are a true believer in hypnosis, there's nothing that can stop you.

You are full of energy and enthusiasm.

Enthusiasm comes from the root word en-theos. This basically means "God Within." The life force, all that is good and powerful in the world, within *you*. And from that place, you are able to do anything that you can conceive of. That is the power of hypnosis, and that is the power of being enthusiastic about the work you do. It is magnetic. People will be *drawn to you*. They will want to work with you because you have something that they want.

> **Professional Hypnotist Truth #9: An exceptional hypnotist is a true believer in hypnosis and uses their own tools of hypnosis and self-hypnosis on themselves to be at 100 percent when working with clients, and on their business.**

JAIME RELEASES OLD ANGER AND FINALLY FEELS AT PEACE [CASE STUDY]

Jaime was fifty-six years old when she arrived for her fourth day of hypnosis training. Her age doesn't matter, except she's been upset with her mother for mistreating her since she was eight years old.

That's forty-eight years of anger.

And she tried everything to fix it.

She's a forgiving and spiritual woman by nature. A healer by nature. She wanted to become a hypnotist to add to the work she does every day as a massage therapist.

Yet, everything she had tried up to that point had not resolved this anger with her mother.

During class, something brought up old feelings of anger and frustration, and Jaime felt those old feelings all over again.

I could tell she was upset, and asked her if she wanted to keep those feelings, or be rid of them?

I want them gone forever, she reported.

I asked her to focus on the feeling in her body, and as she did the feeling grew stronger.

She was already in a state of hypnosis, as she became more emotional and in the present moment.

Using Age Regression, I asked her to follow back her feeling to an earlier time she felt the same way, and she followed it back to an experience with her mother and her brother.

And throughout this experience, Jaime reported having insight about her mother that up to that point, she didn't realize was happening.

"I realize now, that the reason my mother always gave my brother the extra support and not me, is that I didn't need it. I really didn't. Her not helping me made me stronger and more independent. My brother did need extra help. He still needs extra help."

And with additional insight into how that concept unfolded over the course of her whole life and grew into an overwhelming sense of feeling not good enough, paired with significant unfairness and lack of understanding, she transformed her feelings of anger to wisdom and compassion.

Compassion for her mother and her brother.

Her brother had a physical disability and a learning disability. He needed more help.

Her mother could have made better choices. She could have communicated with Jaime why she always seemed to choose her brother over her. She could have told her it was because she was smart and capable. Yet her mother also struggled and did the best she could with what she had.

Wisdom to realize how all that anger and frustration had never helped her. She realized that having that experience there in class was exactly the kind of personal experience with hypnosis she needed in order become an exceptional hypnotist herself.

Jaime became a true believer in hypnosis that day. And it's made all the difference.

Later, she reported how transcending a feeling of anger that had been with her for over forty years was instrumental in her understanding how to help her clients with similar issues.

"I *knew* everything that came up in hypnosis. But hypnosis gave me the clarity to understand how it was impacting me, and how to transform it into something useful. This experience I can share with clients to help them understand the power of hypnosis."

2. ANY PERCEIVED ISSUE IN YOUR PRACTICE MUST BE RESOLVED IN YOU FIRST

Every perceived issue in your practice is **a reflection of your own personal and internal struggle.** Find harmony within yourself first, then the external issues will be easy to resolve, or will resolve themselves.

Graduates in my mentorship program hear me repeat this all the time.

"*This* is the work."

The things that are frustrating. The things that aren't working. If you let them get you down, your practice will suffer. If you point to something external as the issue, your practice will suffer.

Do Your Due Diligence with Perceived Issues

Do your due diligence to understand any issue that comes up in your practice. This means to do the work to investigate anything that could be misleading, confusing, or broken. If it *is* an external issue, for example your website link isn't working, or the phone system you're using is dropping calls – *then fix it. Those are relatively "easy" fixes.*

And yet most hypnotists will stop there. They'll report "I really don't know why no one is signing up for my class. I don't see anything wrong with it."

And they don't realize the issue is in *them*. It is how they *feel* about the situation, and how they feel is being picked up in all the little ways we communicate – from the words on the website, to the videos we share online, to the way we answer the phone and return email messages.

JOHN FINALLY SELLS OUT HIS CLASS [CASE STUDY]

"No one has signed up for my class yet," John reported on a weekly call in my mentorship program, "and I don't know why."

I reviewed the website first - I will always look at my hypnotist's material to see if I can "spot" anything they've overlooked – doing the due diligence.

I reviewed his website, and his email. I didn't see anything noticeably wrong.

I asked John if he wanted to work with me on this now, during the mentorship call, using hypnosis and he said yes.

"John, imagine that someone just signed up for your class and you see the registration email come in, how does that feel?"

"I'm nervous," he started with, "now I really have to do a great job teaching this class, and what if I don't get it right?"

That is what I was looking for with John. He had an internal reason to not sell the class. And in some way, he was blocking it, yet he wasn't consciously aware of it.

"John, let's resolve this issue with feeling nervous about it first. A little nervousness is good – it makes us want to do a good job, too much blocks us from being successful."

"Focus on that feeling of being nervous, it's connected to every other time in your entire life you've ever felt that way, now follow it back to an earlier time."

John reports that he is in school. (He's revivifying an experience using Age Regression while in hypnosis, and it's a powerful way to help our client release erroneous beliefs and emotions.)

He's in front of the class giving a report. He's in third grade with Mrs. Simpson. He makes a mistake – and the entire class laughs, including the teacher.

In this state, it's easy to help John release these old feelings of fear, and anger, and with hypnosis that's exactly what happened.

In the end, John realized it his mistake was kind of funny – yet the teacher and students shouldn't have laughed like they did.

He realized that having *that* experience made him who he is today – compassionate, and never wanting to make others feel bad. He doesn't want to make fun at another's expense.

"John, bring your attention back to that old feeling you were having about your class, the feeling about being nervous. How does it feel now?"

"It's gone," he stated after a moment of reflection. "I feel so much better now."

"Good, *now* imagine a new order comes in for your class, how do you feel now?"

"Excited!! I can see myself in front of the class teaching it. I see the looks on the faces of my students getting relief. It's a great class, and I'm proud of myself. I get a few new clients out of it too!"

Later that day, John reported having two people sign up for his class.

He had fixed his own feelings regarding the class, and after our call, went online and shared an online post about his class. The content in his post reflected how excited he was about the class, and it resonated with potential students, and they signed up.

The question to ask yourself when something isn't working, is one or both the following:

- If there was anything good about this thing not working the way you want, what would it be? *This can get at any underlying secondary reasons for it to fail.*
- Imagine that it's working, how do you feel?

Both of these questions work well on their own; however, in a state of hypnosis, their impact is amplified because it helps us to recognize the underlying reasons we may be blocking our own success.

We want to remove any resistance to being successful.

Any perceived issue in your business, are a reflection of a deeper, internal issue.

Professional Hypnotist Truth #10: Any perceived issues in your practice is a reflection of your own personal struggle and you must work internally on your own issues using hypnosis and self-hypnosis to resolve them in yourself first before they can be resolved in your practice.

---

3. DO YOUR OWN WORK DAILY

The daily work of a professional hypnotist includes exceptional levels of wellness and self-care.

Take care of your body.

Eat healthy, get great sleep, and de-stress using self-hypnosis and other anti-anxiety techniques.

Take care of your mind.

Read things that are delightful, that make your soul smile.

Engage in thoughtful and purposeful discourse with people on topics you care about. If you don't do this already, you can look forward to the following change: as soon as you begin studying to be a hypnotist and learning about the heart, mind, and behavior, the small talk topic that you may be used to talking about will seem boring.

Take care of your emotional state.

Give your mind stillness. Take time to do nothing. Watch leaves fall. Sit on the floor with your dog or cat. Sit near the lake or ocean and just listen to mother nature. Spend time in the forest with the trees and enjoy hearing the sounds and feel of the earth beneath you. Address your emotional needs, if an emotion comes up that you don't like or want to change, do your self-hypnosis on it.

Take care of yourself spiritually.

Spirituality is a belief in something beyond what we can see with our eyes. It's a belief that there is something more, that some part of our energy continues when we pass away from this life.

It's not organized religion.

Honor that belief in you, whatever it is. If your spirituality is the forest, then visit the forest regularly.

If your spirituality is music, then listen to music regularly.

If your spirituality is being kind and compassionate to others, and reading scripture, then do that regularly.

One of the primary issues I've helped clients resolve, is that they are out of alignment with their own beliefs – whatever they are. As a professional hypnotist your role will be to help your clients with their own beliefs. *You will never push your beliefs on your clients.* You will, however, help your clients recognize their own beliefs and get back into alignment with them so they are living in integrity with their own beliefs.

4. CONNECTION WITH YOURSELF FIRST

Before you are able to truly connect with your client at a heart level – you must connect with yourself and stay connected.

This doesn't mean you have to be perfect to be an exceptional hypnotist.

The opposite is often true.

Students arrive at my courses in varying states of discomfort, suffering, frustration, and anger.

Yet they *know* and *believe* there is something more. They've glimpsed the eternal and know they can have access to it. That's why they are there. Hypnosis allows us to tap into the greatest parts of who we are as humans – and as source, if you have those beliefs. That's why they're there, to use that and help others use it as well.

And the first step is to connect with yourself first, daily.

What Does It Mean to "Connect"?

By connecting, I mean to focus and be present. Release anything that is not integral to that moment, allow yourself to drop into a very powerful resourceful state of knowing and feeling, and yes, I mean do some type of self-hypnosis.

How to Connect with Yourself

Do self-hypnosis, or spiritual connection daily with a focus on you – who you are now as a human.

Forgive yourself. Love yourself. Ask more of yourself. Set high expectations, and give yourself the love and grace to make mistakes and move on for the greater good of the human race.

How Do You Know When You're Connected?

You'll feel it. You'll feel on top of your game. Little things won't bother you. The things that used to upset you, don't. You'll see the big picture, and how all those little annoyances of daily life are really there to help you practice your craft – remaining calm in the face of fear and stress. That is what your clients will present to you, and that's what you'll deal with every day.

Excellent hypnosis work happens organically when you are connected first to yourself, then to your client.

Professional Hypnotist Truth #11: Excellent hypnosis work happens organically when you are connected first to yourself, then to your client. You know you are connected and in alignment with your higher self because you'll feel great, and little things won't bother you.

---

5. LOVE IS ALWAYS THE ANSWER

No matter what you are feeling, love is always the answer. If you're frustrated by a situation at your current job, love is the answer.

Hurt people, hurt people.

When others are hurting, they behave badly out of fear and anxiety, and anger, and other negative feelings, and it comes to bear on us and our lives.

Love them anyway.

Every single day, make it your mission to not only love when it is easy, but love when it is hard.

It's easy to love something that we already perceive as being *good*. It's easy to love a loving and caring person.

I want you to love when it is hard.

Find a way to love people who are suffering., who behave badly, and who aren't nice. Find a way to love them, starting with loving yourself.

By challenging yourself to love when it is hard, you increase your capacity for love, which positively connects you to every area of your life, including self-care and your work as a hypnotist.

> Challenge yourself to increase your capacity to love every single day by loving not only when it is easy, but by loving when it is *hard*.

> *Professional Hypnotist Truth #12: Find something in a negative situation to love - so that you can connect. Find something in a 'bad' behavior to love so that you can connect, starting with yourself. There is always a good reason to continue with a bad behavior, it just may not be a good enough reason.*

HEATHER HEALS A LIFELONG ISSUE WITH HER SISTER [CASE STUDY]

Heather was a student in my hypnosis certification training course. She asked how she could possibly love her sister who had willfully and purposefully bullied her as a child, then manipulated her and caused significant stress in her life as an adult.

"It's always been this way. We just butt heads. She has to be right, and everyone, not just me, is always wrong."

I asked Heather if she wanted to be rid of that feeling she had toward her sister, or if she'd rather keep it?

"I want to be rid of it, but I've already tried that dozens of times."

I helped Heather enter into hypnosis with an affect-based hypnosis induction.

Once there, I asked her to imagine her relationship with her sister, and what it felt *like.*

"We're in constant conflict, it's like two rams constantly butting heads, over and over."

"And how do you *want* it to be instead? What is that *like*?"

"I don't even want to butt heads anymore, about anything. I don't even want to play this game! I want to be free. I want to be like the wind, I can go wherever I want, and my sister can fight with someone else if she wants."

"Good," I reply. "Imagine that, imagine you're no longer the ram. What's happening now?"

Laughing, Heather said, "My sister isn't the ram either, it was just a front. She's scared, she's putting up a show. She turned into a bird, and she's sailing on the wind, I'm lifting her up and she's gliding and swooping. We're doing it together."

After finishing up work with Heather on this issue, she reported that *during* the hypnosis her sister had texted her saying, "Hey, what are you up to?"

And Heather was dumfounded. "My sister never texts me to check in. *Ever.*"

Their relationship hasn't resolved itself entirely, but it has improved.

CHALLENGE YOURSELF TO LOVE WHEN IT IS HARD, AND WATCH THE MAGIC UNFOLD.

When there is nothing to resist against (meaning you offer only love – not resistance), the other party has nothing to push against. And they have to change course.

Try it now:

Make a fist with both of your hands and press them against each other in opposing directions. If each hand is pressing with the same force, nothing will move. You'll just get a little workout.

Now, with one of your hands, collapse your fist, and remove resistance entirely.

The other hand has no choice but to shift, to move. There's nothing to push against. It has to move, or also stop resisting. The same is true for emotional and spiritual shifts as well.

By using hypnosis to remove resistance, and transform negative energy to only love, the shift in energy can create amazing new dynamics that lead to powerful shifts in relationships – even if the relationships are decades old.

I've used this technique in session with clients and students dozens of times, and it always creates a positive shift in their relationship. It's not all that is required, but it often serves as a catalyst to move the needle in a desired direction – even if the relationship has been at a standstill for decades.

Never underestimate the power you have in your own ability to be kind and loving, and what it can bring to the world.

HIGH PERFORMANCE HYPNOSIS

High Performance Hypnosis is a method and a model for entrepreneurs, hypnotists, and anyone who wants a high performance life. These are the tools I use with my clients, hypnosis students, and graduates to help them get exceptional results. This book is not about high performance hypnosis, but here's an overview of what it entails.

Here's an overview of the framework:

Energy: Tools to Relax, Motivate, Recharge, and Transform.

Tools using hypnosis and self-hypnosis to increase energy and motivation, and bring calm and stillness. Strategies to respond appropriately to situations, with repetition and expectation.

Create: Tools to Change, Expand, and Grow

Tools to accelerate learning, think multi-dimensionally, to transfer expertise, facilitate sublime experiences, and transcend the abyss.

Attention: Tools to Focus

Tools that provide clarity and vision, to bring balance.

For information on _High Performance Hypnosis_, visit the additional tools offered as part of this book at **_CanYouBeAHypnotist. com._**

These tools all use hypnosis as the basis for making accelerated changes in each direction, so hypnosis is the foundation.

Now that you've learned the top ten hypnosis techniques and know what you need to do for yourself to be an exception hypnotist – you are ready to learn what it will take to grow your business.

The next chapter is on Growing Your Business, and the top 4 steps to having a thriving hypnosis practice in six months.

CHAPTER SIX
BUSINESS SKILLS

"Between stimulus and response there is a space. In that space is our power to choose our response. In our response lies our growth and our freedom."
– VIKTOR FRANKL

Having the skills of a master hypnotist and being in personal alignment aren't enough to have a thriving hypnosis practice.

You also need the business skills to grow your practice.

If you're not thrilled about this part of becoming a hypnotist, you're not alone. Many hypnosis practices fail because the hypnotist ignores this critical aspect of their business.

And the good news is that if you have the proper hypnosis skills, and use them to stay in personal alignment, then this part *can* be easy.

Instead of feeling overwhelmed with too much to do, the professional hypnotist will use a relaxation and focusing technique to gain clarity on what to do next – realizing it will all get done in time. Knowing everything always works out.

Instead of feeling nervous about talking with a potential new client, the professional hypnotist will use self-hypnosis to build confidence and focus on staying fully present and connecting with their new client.

Instead of being worried about what to do next, the professional hypnotist with a systematic approach built into their practice will *know* exactly what to do. They'll be focused and calm. And if there is anything unclear, they will use self-hypnosis and other tools as a hypnotist to gain clarity and alignment on the next steps.

Why Hypnotists Fail to Grow Their Practice

The primary reasons hypnotists fail to grow their practice include:

THEY DON'T REALIZE THE IMPORTANCE OF MARKETING

- They misunderstand the value and necessity of marketing themselves and their services. They believe that clients should somehow just "find" them.
- They don't like some types of marketing and don't realize they can market in a way that feels good to them.
- Some hypnotists desire the elusive "referral only" type of practice they heard of. A referral only method is possible to achieve. However, it can take many years and enough clients to build a referral only practice. And you will not be serving some

of your most needed clients this way either – some will never find you if your business is referral-only. Marketing allows us to reach clients who need us, yet aren't familiar with how hypnosis can help them.

THEY DON'T HAVE THE BUSINESS SKILLS OR OPERATIONAL SYSTEMS TO SUPPORT PRACTICE GROWTH

- They don't know basic business building strategies and get overwhelmed by trying to work on too many things at once. The solution is to know precisely what to focus on and in what order to bring in business and grow their practice. We can't do everything at once, yet it all will get done in time. Knowing what and when is key.
- They don't have a systematic approach to helping clients and create one-off solutions for every client which quickly becomes overwhelming.
- They don't have operational elements to simplify and focus on the right aspects to grow successfully.

THEY'RE INSECURE ABOUT HYPNOSIS SKILLS AND MONEY

- They are insecure about their own worth and skills as a hypnotist, and have a hard time asking for money for their services, and often undercharge which stunts growth.
- Excellent hypnosis training is the foundation of hypnosis mastery and practice success. Beyond that, the hypnotist must use their own skills as a hypnotist with personal alignment to ensure they're not blocking their own progress with feelings of insecurity, or money blocks.

4 Keys to Building a Successful Hypnosis Practice

These are the foundational business elements of growing a successful and thriving hypnotherapy practice.

1. GENERATE AWARENESS WITH AN AWARENESS STRATEGY

An awareness strategy is how people you don't know become aware of your business. This includes marketing your hypnosis services, which is really offering a **solution to their issue.**

Professional hypnotists don't focus on offering hypnosis; rather we focus on *offering solutions to our client's problems.*

Professional Hypnotist Truth #13: Offer a solution to your potential client that solves their problem.

We are offering our clients results. A solution to their problem. We don't focus on hypnosis. Hypnosis is the method; the results are what our clients want. For example, your clients likely don't care what type of hypnosis you use, or the hypnotherapeutic techniques you offer. They want to know "Will this solve my problem?"

A good awareness strategy helps our potential clients know that we will help them solve their problem.

For new hypnotists, it's common to work with friends or family initially, but very quickly you'll need a new batch of potential clients every month. Part of what makes hypnosis so attractive for our clients is we deliver results in a short amount of time - on average we work with our clients for five sessions. This means that needing new clients every month is a natural part of our business model.

It's common for new practitioners, and new entrepreneurs, to want to try "everything and see what sticks," regarding marketing, but this strategy is not effective.

If you put ten percent of your time and energy into ten different things, you'll likely get a ten percent result on all of them and feel as if nothing worked.

Instead, implement the following strategy.

How to decide on an awareness strategy: Focus on *one* thing at a time and get *good* at it, then add in new strategies.

Deciding on what to focus on first to bring in new business can be challenging for new hypnotists because they're often so excited to get started helping people they want to do everything all at once. Yet it doesn't have to be challenging at all when done well.

The following question is designed to help you understand what awareness strategy may be best for you.

How did you become aware of hypnosis, and then hypnosis training, or this book, in the first place?

This will help you understand *what awareness strategy worked for you* that you may want to implement in your practice.

• Download your Awareness Strategy Worksheet online at **CanYouBeAHypntosit.com.**

2. IDENTIFY AND ATTRACT YOUR IDEAL CLIENT

Identifying an ideal client for your practice brings clarity and effective communication to attract the *right clients* to your practice.

My ideal hypnosis client is Mary. Mary is a specific person with a particular issue. Mary is forty-nine years old and wants to lose weight. She feels out of control in her life because of sugar and overeating. Mary is smart, and successful in every area of her life except weight loss. She works as an office manager at a large retail store. She's tried everything to lose weight yet has been unsuccessful for the last thirty years.

When I think of Mary, I imagine her in a dark room, with the television on. She's crying. She just finished another half-gallon of her favorite ice cream, yet she still doesn't feel satisfied. Instead, she feels distraught. She feels like a failure and is desperate for change. Mary grabs her phone, and with a last bit of hope, types "help with weight loss" into her browser. My business appears top on the list of search results "Lose Weight with Hypnosis, Proven and Effective. Call to Schedule Your Complimentary Consultation Now."

Mary calls and schedules her consultation, and I get the honor of helping her lose weight and keep it off, for life.

Identifying and attracting your ideal client is *not* "niching" down your practice. We are not eliminating issues for you to help with. You may have multiple ideal clients that you love working with. The goal is to understand your client's problem so you can focus your marketing efforts and communicate with them appropriately.

When done well, your client will say to you *"You were talking to me!"* when referring to the article you wrote, or the ad that attracted them, or the podcast they heard you on.

The Key to Identifying Your Ideal Client Is to Be Specific

The more you understand your ideal client, including their issue and what they want, the more likely they will be drawn to working with you.

You may be wondering how identifying one ideal client with a very specific job, and a very specific issue can help grow your practice? Taking Mary as an example, how many women aged forty-nine with a job as an office manager want to lose weight?

There are *thousands.*

Thousands who identify with Mary's story. Thousands who, when they read or hear your story about Mary will identify with her situation. Our brains are good at pattern matching and making generalizations, so even though Mary is an office manager, a man working at the bank will identify with Mary's frustration and feelings of inadequacy. A woman working as a hospice nurse will resonate with Mary's inability to eat healthy at the end of the day.

Specificity is the key because in making the story specific, Mary becomes a *real person with real issues.* Potential clients will think 'you're talking to me'.

While Specificity is the key, it's a means to the end result which is the ability for you – the hypnotist, to **love your client before you even meet them.**

"Find a way to Love Every Client that walks through the door" - Cal Banyan

Professional Hypnotist Truth #14: Find a way to love every single client that you work with.

Remember - our clients don't come to us because they feel well. They come to us seeking respite, comfort and relief from their struggles.

They've tried everything, and it hasn't worked. Our clients come to us with behaviors they want to be rid of. With fears holding them back, and these fears and behaviors will be a part of working with them.

This is why it is so important to learn to love when it is hard. Every day, our job is to learn to love greater than the day before. Find a way to love every single client, then get them the results they came in for.

STEPS TO IDENTIFY YOUR IDEAL CLIENT

This format works well all on its own, but it's super-charged while in a state of hypnosis. This format is an adapted version of what my publisher, Angela Lauria, teaches when writing a book to an ideal reader, and here it is modified for hypnosis and our ideal clients.

1. Write down your ideal client's problems, in their words.

I'm tired of feeling so heavy.
My eating is out of control.

I want to stop smoking so I can spend more time with my grandkids.
If I don't stop drinking, I'm going to lose everything.

2. Write down their dream come true, in their words.

I fit into my favorite jeans and am hiking with my son and granddaughter.
I'm traveling more because I can easily fit into every seat!
I haven't smoked in a year, and instead, have watched my grandson Bobby become a great soccer player!
I haven't had a drink in 6 months, and I'm happy to be creating music again!

3. What does your ideal client look like?

While in hypnosis, imagine what your client looks like, including the expression on their face. What are they wearing? What are they doing? What are they saying? What are they feeling? What does she hear in her head?

Mary is forty-nine years old, and she looks exhausted. She's wearing baggy clothing with a scarf. She's at the grocery store, desperately trying to avoid buying her favorite chips and cookies, feeling out of control, and inadequate. She says to herself, tomorrow is going to be better.

4. What are they searching online for?

What does your ideal client search for online to solve their problem before finding you? What else have they tried?

Mary searches for "alternative weight loss," "sugar addiction," and maybe even "hypnosis for weight loss."

5. Write up a short synopsis of your ideal client

This is a loving piece of work you are doing for your client. You are connecting to your client in a state of hypnosis to understand their pain points and their dream come true. Genuinely caring about how to reach them and help them solve their problem with hypnosis.

You are getting into an energetic state where you are sending out a beacon of hope to your ideal clients, with love in your heart saying "I can help you" to the universe. Your ideal clients will be pulled into your business like a magnet – they will be drawn to work with you. And it's all because you took the time and energy to truly understand their issue, then did everything you could to help them know that you also had a solution to their problem. You made the issue personal to them. And they felt heard and understood. They believe that you can help them.

You can run your entire business by serving one ideal client. However, I recommend having a minimum of 3 to begin working with. It's common to have your ideal client *find you*. So your initial ideas about who you want to work with will shift over time.

6. Update Regularly

As you continue working with your ideal clients, update your ideal client worksheet. The better you get at knowing your ideal client, the easier it will be for you to help them and get them massive results. This should be a document and exercise you return to regularly, at least once a month.

- Download your Ideal Client Worksheet online at *CanYouBeAHypntosit.com.*

3. TALK ABOUT WHAT YOU DO

Talking about what you do may be number three on this list; however, it is the number one way to reach your ideal clients.

Talk about what you do.

Talk verbally, write about it, create videos on hypnosis. Share stories.

Professional Hypnotist Truth #15: The more you talk about what you do as a hypnotist and how it can help people, the more successful you will be.

Our clients want to know that hypnosis will solve their problem, and they want to know it's safe and not a scam. There are too many misperceptions about hypnosis. We – professional hypnotists – must be out there in the world sharing and telling compelling stories about how hypnosis works, that it's safe, effective and natural, and precisely what hypnosis helps with.

Tell everyone you know that you are a hypnotist and that you help clients even when everything else has failed.

Repeatedly communicate the benefits of hypnosis and the issues it helps with.

Share stories of client success, and teach classes on hypnosis, self-hypnosis, and other related topics.

I have my students start talking about becoming a hypnotist

before they even arrive at training. By the time they graduate, they already have their first clients lined up to work with them.

There is so much misunderstanding in the world about hypnosis. It is critical that we talk about the what hypnosis really is, and the benefits it provides.

HERE ARE THE FOUR PRIMARY CORNERSTONES OF TALKING ABOUT WHAT YOU DO

Within the first year of hypnosis, I want all of my grads to have completed all of the following:

1. **The Hypnosis Pre-Talk**
   Answers the question: What is hypnosis?

The hypnosis pre-talk is the talk we give every new hypnosis client. It includes what hypnosis actually is, and eliminates common fears and misperceptions about hypnosis. You are likely to give this pre-talk in a variety of lengths and formats throughout your career as a professional hypnotist.

2. **Short Elevator Pitch**
   Answers the question: What do you do?

The short elevator pitch is a one-sentence description of what you do.

Here's mine: "I'm a hypnotist. I help people lose weight, with hypnosis – even when everything else has failed."

And when I'm talking to potential students, "I'm an award-winning hypnotherapy trainer and author. I train compassionate humans to become world-class hypnotists with a thriving practice, without the struggle."

The format is the following:
I am a _____, I help people _____ [even when or without] _____.

I'm a hypnotist. I help people with hypnosis, even when everything else has failed.

This format includes adaptations from both Cal Banyan and my speaking coach Majeed Mogharreban.

3. **Entry Level, Community-Based Course**
Answers the question: How can hypnosis benefit me?

Teach an entry level course that includes hypnosis that is appropriate for your community. This course will include a Hypnosis Pre-talk, mentioned earlier, to help students understand what hypnosis is. This is yet another reason why having a Hypnosis Pre-talk is essential – you'll use it in public speaking and while teaching classes as well.

It's important that it's an entry-level course so that *anyone – even without any experience with hypnosis, can get something out of it.*

It's important that it's community-based because it should be something your community – or a collection of your ideal clients, would be interested in.

Some examples include the following:
· Introduction to Self-Hypnosis

- Stress Buster Workshop
- Can Hypnosis Help with Weight Loss?
- Can Hypnosis Help to Stop Smoking?

4. *Client Success*

Tell compelling success stories of your clients. Get permission to share their story - either anonymously, or with their names - online, in print, in video, and on your website.

Before you have worked with any clients, there are still plenty of compelling stories to tell your clients. They are my stories. They are other hypnotist's stories. Borrow from my success.

You say, "My colleague worked with a client who wanted to lose weight. Her name was Mary...."

Words alone don't heal, it's the sentiment: the underlying and connecting elements. We must tell compelling stories to help our clients make the change they want to make.

Professional Hypnotist Truth #16: Share compelling stories that your client can connect with to help them.

Professional hypnotists use language and words to help our clients. Yet words alone aren't enough. We are more likely to help our clients with compelling stories that communicate ideas and evoke powerful emotions.

Our clients come to us with their own stories. Stories that include limitations, and erroneous elements. We will help them re-write and create a new, hopeful, and powerful story that helps them obtain the success they desire.

> *We share stories of success* with our clients to help them understand how hypnosis can help them, and also stories that demonstrate how they can feel and be different.

A master hypnotist is also a master storyteller. The stories use hypnotic language that makes the stories captivating and include emotional elements that generate desire and cause powerful shifts in our clients.

4.   SIMPLIFY: CREATE REPEATABLE OFFERINGS THAT FOCUS ON RESULTS

Your Awareness Strategy will attract your *Ideal Client*, and you connect with and listen to your client to understand their issue. Then you will *Talk About What You Do* to help them learn how hypnosis will help to solve their problem.

The last step is getting your client to sign up to work with you and getting them their results.

Client Conversion Funnel

A Client Conversion Funnel is how we will convert a potential client, into a paying client. If this topic makes you feel uncomfortable, then just know that there may be money or money block issues for you to address.

We are of highest service to our clients when they trust in us, and ultimately themselves, enough to pay to have their issue resolved.

And a thriving hypnosis practice means:

- Clients are getting the results they came in for, and they'll tell their friends and our business will grow.
- The Business is able to reinvest in the business - in book publishing, product development, training, and hiring.
- The hypnotist has all their financial needs met and is able to travel, take time off, and afford to take excellent care of themselves and their family.

Steps in the Client Conversion Funnel

Step 1: Sign Up for Complimentary Consultation. Your Awareness Strategy focuses on your Ideal Client. It attracts your ideal client, and they like what you have to say. They sign up for a complimentary consultation with you. The consultation can be over the phone, the internet, or in person.

Step 2: Complimentary Consultation. The complimentary consultation is where you listen and connect with your potential client, then tell them about hypnosis and how it can solve their problem.

Step 3: Make an Offer. If you believe hypnosis can help them, then you will make them an offer to work with you. If they also think it will solve their problem, they will pay you to help them. When this is done well, it works. It feels right, and it feels natural, because you have done the hard work to identify your ideal client and to help them become aware of your services in order to solve their problem. The last step is simply describing how, specifically, hypnosis can help solve their problem.

The Offer Should be Four or More Hypnosis Sessions

The offer will be a package of hypnosis sessions, customized for every client based on their needs. However, we can only ever offer an estimate, an average based on experience with other clients that have similar issues. Each client is different, so there is no way to know for certain how many sessions it will take to help our clients get the results they want.

What about the Miraculous 'Single' Hypnosis Session?

You may be aware of some hypnotists who claim to offer results in a single session. And I don't want you to be that hypnotist. I want you to do complete and thorough work with your clients.

And while it's possible to get our clients fantastic results in a single session, it's not likely to do *complete* work.

Most of our clients have been suffering from their issue for years, maybe decades or more. So even though a single hypnosis session can shift everything for them, it's unlikely to be enough to help them be 100 percent successful.

It can be the turning point to a new life. It can be miraculous.

Even with all of that, our clients may struggle with integrating their new understanding into their current life.

We do not do any service to our clients by offering "Single session cures." If the hypnosis we offer truly is that miraculous, then at least work with your client a minimum of four sessions to ensure they integrate those changes successfully into their life. Otherwise, a month later your single session cure client may think "Oh, I guess hypnosis doesn't work, after all." And that's not good for your client, or for you or your business.

Love your clients enough to make them a thoughtful and thorough offer – not one that makes them feel better at that moment, but one that actually gets them results.

Professional Hypnotist Truth #17: It takes multiple hypnosis sessions to truly help our clients.

Single session miracles are a myth. How do you know if your client got their results if you only see them one time?

Don't jump on this marketing bandwagon. Love your client enough to know it will take multiple sessions to help them with issues they've been struggling with for years, maybe decades.

We can offer significant insight and relief in a single session, this is true. Integrating it back into their existing life can take time, and multiple sessions are required for that.

Don't do what sounds good to your client in the moment – offer them what you know will work in the long run.

Putting It All Together

A professional hypnotist with a thriving practice is:

- A **Master Hypnotist** and knows how to use the modern and professional techniques that are most effective to bring clients results.
- In **Personal Alignment** and uses his or her own hypnosis techniques to operate at 100 percent as often as possible, with a goal of approaching self-actualization.
- Has **Business Skills** and knows how to attract and convert the *right* clients to get them outstanding results. The business grows as a result of client success.

Now that you know what do to, it's equally important to know what to avoid. The next chapter is on the Common Mistakes to Avoid to Accelerate Your Hypnosis Practice.

CHAPTER SEVEN

AVOID THESE COMMON MISTAKES TO ACCELERATE YOUR PRACTICE

"I never lose – I either win, or I learn."

– NELSON MANDELA

There are obstacles to starting anything new, to creating something bold, to stepping out into the unknown for the greater good.

And, yes, there will be challenges when starting your new hypnosis practice or adding hypnosis to your existing practice.

And you can accelerate your practice by avoiding these common mistakes.

However, before we begin, consider the nature, the purpose of mistakes – or what I call mis-takes.

Perceived Mis-Takes and Failing Fast

A mistake is merely a *mis*-take. It's as if in a rehearsal for a live show or performance, the practice (the take, as in take one, take two) was not done quite as well as it could have been. This is why we practice. This is why it's important to rehearse the hypnotic induction over and over, so it becomes so familiar to your mind that it rolls off your tongue, and you are fully present with your client.

Keep in mind one of my favorite quotes attributed to Nelson Mandela: "I never lose – I either win, or I learn."

When we make a perceived *mis*-take, please take a moment, and ask yourself the following, "If I could do this all over again, would I do it any different?" and if the answer is yes, then please know that this is a natural part of the learning process. This is how we can learn and grow so quickly.

I first learned the concept of *failing fast* when I was working in computing as a software engineer. Before failing fast, engineers and programmers would work on projects for months at a time before requesting feedback from the stakeholders – those paying for the software.

This became quite a problem, as there were times when the software built was not what the stakeholder wanted.

Yet three months had passed, and significant money and effort had been placed into this project.

Instead, a new paradigm was introduced, today called Agile or Lean programming. The idea is to work on something for a shorter period of time and get stakeholder input. If the stakeholders didn't like what we created in two weeks, we'd rather know early.

This concept became known as *fail fast*.

Successful entrepreneurs, business owners, and hypnotists aren't perfect – or even smarter. They get excellent training, do their own internal work, learn the business skills, then recognize when something isn't working, and *adapt and make adjustments*. They *fail fast*.

Here are the top six mis-takes to learn from now, and avoid to accelerate your practice:

1. THINKING YOU HAVE TO HAVE A HYPNOSIS SCRIPT FOR EVERYTHING

Hypnosis scripts are valuable for the new hypnotist, and for learning in general. They can help you understand how someone else conceived of and considered a solution to an issue your client may also be having.

However, too many hypnotists rely heavily on scripts written by someone else, that don't actually apply to their client.

Read scripts and learn from them. Then write your own in your own words, using your own language and tone. If a hypnosis script is written by another hypnotist, it will be using their words and tone. It's harder to be congruent if you're using someone else's unmodified work.

Here's how to make good use of a hypnosis script in session with clients:

1. **Read the script and learn from it.**
   Make a note of what resonates with you. Read multiple scripts from different practitioners.

2. **Write your own version, using your own language.**
   Or modify the existing script to a large enough degree that it becomes "yours." This script will be congruent with who you are as a person and hypnotist, and it will have a more positive impact on your client.

3. **In session, be fully present with your client.**
   Use the insight generating techniques discussed in chapter 4. In most cases, you will not read them your script! Instead, you will deliver portions of it, at the right time during the hypnosis session.

Always write down your clients verbalized hypnotic suggestions.

Professional Hypnotist Truth #18: Always write down hypnotic suggestions your clients share with you.

They may not realize they are sharing hypnotic suggestions with you – but as a professional hypnotist, you will recognize them and their power.

Then, during the hypnosis session repeat your client's own words back to them.

In a deep state of hypnosis, the suggestion will sink into your client's heart and mind completely.

Your client will tell you that was the most beautiful thing they've ever heard, not always recalling they were the ones that first said it to you.

THE BEST HYPNOSIS SUGGESTIONS COME FROM YOUR CLIENTS

A hypnosis script is really a method for delivering hypnosis suggestions. And the best hypnosis suggestions come from your client. This was briefly covered in chapter 4 on the Most Powerful Hypnotic Words, but here is more detail.

For example, Lori came to me to lose weight.

On her first hypnosis session, she said to me "I just don't want to think about food anymore."

I wrote that down, verbatim.

Later, in the hypnosis session, Lori had significant insight as to why she had been unable to lose weight and keep it off. She felt lighter and released limiting beliefs about herself as a writer, and a mother.

I said to her, "And now because of these insights, you realize *you just don't want to think about food anymore. And it's easy for you to do so. Instead, you're thinking of all the other things that are important to you – your writing, your daughter, the characters in your stories.*"

After the session, Lori told me that when I said to her "you just don't want to think about food anymore," it *really* sunk in, and she felt the difference.

The next week she came in for her third session and reported that she hardly thought about food all week long. She was more peaceful and happy than she'd been in a long time, and her life seemed richer – fuller because she was focused on other things that were more important to her.

Never underestimate the resiliency of the human spirit.

Professional Hypnotist Truth #19: Never underestimate the resiliency of the human spirit. Believe in your clients beyond anything they can imagine. Hold that belief, polish it up. Make it shine.

For all of our faults and shortcomings as humans, we are incredible creatures with abilities that go way beyond our current understanding of possibility.

---

2. UNDERESTIMATING HOW IMPORTANT MARKETING AND SALES ARE

Marketing is helping people become aware of your business, sales is when you actually exchange money when a client chooses to work with you.

Both are important, and both are necessary. If you don't have any experience in either, you will need to. And I don't think this is part of your business that you should simply pay others to do without also understanding it yourself.

The reason is that it is so important to the ongoing success of your practice. And marketing and selling your services are an intimate and personal element of your business.

If you copy what someone else is doing, it doesn't feel congruent.

If you don't market your business with love and care for your clients, you'll attract the wrong people.

If you don't know how to sell your services, clients won't understand why they should work with you.

Here are the rules for marketing and sales:

- Marketing is helping others become aware of your services. This is required. It's the awareness strategy covered in chapter 7. Do it with love and care. Base it on your ideal client.

- Imagine that your ideal client is going to continue to suffer from their issue until you reach them, somehow. Until they read your blog post. Until they hear your podcast or until they see your advertisement. *We have to be courageous in our attempts to reach our ideal clients. We at times do things that feel uncomfortable, so that our clients can see our message of hope, connect with us, and work with us. We go into the dark, scary places that require courage and grit first, for the things that scare us as hypnotists, as humans. Then our clients can follow our lead and the path we've illuminated.*

- Sales are about helping your client envision a better version of themselves. It's not about hypnosis. It's not how great you are as a hypnotist or all of the certificates you have or awards you've won. It's very simply, can this solve their problem? And if so, what does it look like? Help your client envision their best self, their better future, then tell them how you are going to *help empower them* to get there.

- Don't ever do anything with Sales and Marketing your business that feels bad to you. If you get a negative gut reaction to something, fix it. Listen to your inner wisdom.

> We are *selling* a better version of our client to themselves. We're not selling hypnosis.
>
> ***Professional Hypnotist Truth #20: Your job is to help your client envision a brighter future, their best self. That is what you are selling to them.***

Sales are about helping your client envision a better version of themselves.

It's not about hypnosis.

It's not how great you are as a hypnotist or all of the certificates you have or awards you've won.

It's very simply, can this solve their problem? And if so, what does it look like? Help your client envision their best self, their better future, then tell them how you are going to help empower them to get there.

3. NOT HAVING A SYSTEMATIC APPROACH

Having a systematic approach for your hypnosis practice means you *know* what to do with each client and are not reinventing your practice or approach with every new client.

I witness many hypnotists struggle with this. And thankfully some of them then end up training with me for this very reason. Being an entrepreneur and setting your own schedule, while helping people is very fulfilling and rewarding, and it's also hard work.

Without systems in place to understand what to do for the first session of hypnosis, every new client will be a struggle.

Without systems in place to understand what to do when your client wants to lose weight, or stop smoking, or eliminate other bad habits, you'll find you're working too hard for each individual client.

Instead, a systematic approach allows you to do great work with *every single client* because you are repeating techniques and processes that have worked for thousands of hypnotists and thousands of clients.

Those techniques and processes become the foundation of the work you do. Then with each individual client, your approach shifts slightly. You have the foundation and most powerful techniques as part of your system, which you use in a custom way for each client. It's the perfect mix of custom and reusable, effective techniques.

STEVE'S STORY: FROM TECH EXECUTIVE TO PROFESSIONAL HYPNOTIST WITH A THRIVING PRACTICE

Steve had always been interested in healing, the mind, and alternative medicine. Eighteen years ago, while studying acupuncture and herbal medicine, he got lured away by the internet boom. He spent the better part of the last two decades building a great career in tech – but it wasn't enough.

His heart needed the satisfaction of helping people in a tangible way. After finding personal help with hypnosis, he knew what he had to do. He took a leap of faith, got training and certification, and hasn't looked back.

Steve followed a systematic approach in getting excellent training and certification to launch his hypnosis practice, and that's the foundation of what made his business successful right away.

Within two weeks of graduating from the class, Steve had his entire business set up.

He rented an office, moved in the furniture he needed, bought a recliner, and had a website set up. The biggest puzzle piece for Steve was getting new clients. As soon as he figured that out and had people coming to his website, he started getting booked for consultations.

Steve said, "There's nothing like having your first consultation scheduled for a Monday morning to motivate you over the weekend to finish getting your office set up. As soon as I had that first consult and signed that person as a client, I knew that everything was going to work. My training had prepared me to see real clients—and now I had proved to myself that they would come. I have never looked back!"

His mission is to help other people who are at that precipice of change in their own lives to realize that not only is it safe to jump – but that they can fly!

4. LETTING CLIENTS RUN THEIR SESSIONS

Don't let your clients run the session. If our clients knew how to solve their own problems, they wouldn't come to see us. So, it's critical that you are in charge of your client session.

What does this really mean?
- Don't allow your client to tell you what techniques they want you to use, or what to work on for that day.
- Don't change your regular appointment time to accommodate their schedule.
- Don't allow them to reschedule sessions outside a strict appointment policy (at least five business days). It's not feasible for you to run a business where clients are rescheduling with less than a week to fill an appointment slot. As a rule, you will

not be overfilling your appointment calendar similar to a typical doctor's office. Don't make your clients wait. Instead, each client should get your full attention for a full amount of time — at least 90 minutes. This gets our clients fantastic results! And to do that, their part is to show up at the scheduled time.

Don't allow your client to tell you what to focus on for that day, or what technique to use in session. You are in charge. With a systematic approach, you will have a plan for the day. And depending on what your client reports in the pre-hypnosis interview, your plans may change. But they are your plans. Allowing your clients to depict what to focus on and what techniques to use is a big mistake that does not get our clients results. Keep in mind that our clients will often request to work on elements that may *seem entirely valid*. Yet what you'll learn as you gain more experience, is that we'll often desire to work on something that is not our primary issue, to protect ourselves. Don't allow this to happen in your practice.

A common way this shows up in session is when clients ask to shift appointment times or reschedule their sessions. I highly recommend that you have a strict appointment policy and have set times and days that you work. If you adjust your schedule to meet your client's needs, it does not help them.

For example, when I was a new hypnotist, I had a client who wanted to come in at eleven-thirty instead of my regular eleven a.m. appointment. Not realizing why it was essential to have them stick with my timeframe, I allowed this client to make adjustments to my schedule. I compromised and said it would be alright if they came in at eleven-thirty instead of eleven. When the day of the appointment arrived, the client showed up at twelve instead, and we only completed a partial session. On top of that, I didn't get to work with a one p.m. client either, because I had agreed to adjust my schedule. In the end, instead of two full hypnosis sessions, I was only able to complete one partial session.

DAVID'S STORY: AN EXECUTIVE COACH INCORPORATES HYPNOSIS FOR EVEN BETTER RESULTS

David is an executive level coach – he coaches CEO's of major corporations. He's excellent at what he does, and part of his process is always incorporating new methods to get even better results for his clients.

Once David incorporated hypnosis into his coaching practice, he realized he had the ability to show clients how to set high expectations and boundaries with themselves on purpose in order to reveal any lingering subconscious limiting beliefs. Here's what he had to say about hypnosis:

"I've been an executive coach working with CEOs, C-level Executives, and Entrepreneurs for over fifteen years. A big part of effective coaching is helping the client identify and reframe limiting beliefs and blindspots. I also have observed a consistent pattern where intellectual solutions to problems do not always work. In those cases, the client creates an action plan, but then does not execute on it and sometimes works directly against it. Some call that self-sabotage, but I call it self-protection. I incorporated hypnosis into my practice for one simple reason -- efficiency and time to results. Conventional coaching often would take a very long time to surface the limiting beliefs and self-protective behaviors, and then the methods to change them were cognitive. I now use hypnosis as part of an integrated approach to ensure that the client's internal subconscious mindset is very clear and that the change is enduring."

Set strict boundaries and high expectations for your clients. The boundaries will help your clients be accountable.

Professional Hypnotist Truth #21: Set strict boundaries for your clients with high expectations. The boundaries and expectations keep our clients accountable and get better results.

Don't make adjustments to your calendar for your clients. Have them meet your availability. If you give in to their demands, they are now running the show, and everything you do with them will be harder. Remember, they're coming to you for help.

Help them first, by setting expectations of when and where to meet and have strict appointment policies to keep them accountable. Having your clients show up to session is a critical part of getting them the relief and results they desire.

Most of our clients are stressed and busy! And without the strict guidelines, many will just make more excuses as to why that day they were too busy or stressed to come to session.

5. FOCUSING ON NON-REVENUE GENERATING TASKS

Anytime a professional hypnotist is not working with clients, the next task they should be focusing on is bringing in new clients. And that is done with an effective Awareness Strategy (discussed in chapter 5).

However, many hypnotists would rather update their website, or brochure, or get new headshots, then do the work of bringing in new business.

Don't make this mistake. New hypnotists should be focused on bringing in new clients.

STEVEN LOVES SHOPPING FOR HIS NEW OFFICE

Steve graduated from hypnosis certification training and quickly began looking for a new office. He was excited and looking forward to his new career helping people.

He mentioned that he didn't want to sign up new clients yet because he didn't have an office.

I advised him to sign up clients. The office will come.

And sure enough, he signed up a new client – no office.

In two days, he had an office.

Don't get caught up in non-revenue generating tasks.

Professional Hypnotist Truth #22: When you're not in front of a client, focus on revenue generating tasks – which means getting new clients.

It's tempting to want to read that new book or redesign the website. Yet if you haven't met your monthly sales goals, your primary task needs to be talking to clients. Your initial goal as a new hypnotist is to create a consistent stream of new clients with an awareness strategy that works month over month.

These other tasks are important, yet they're supportive. They

---

are not primary. Focus on the primary tasks first. Primary tasks include scheduling complimentary consultations, direct outreach to potential clients, answering the phone, signing up new clients, and making offers online in video, or sending emails with offers.

In the story below, Michael quickly discovered that his hypnosis practice and revenue generating opportunities extended way beyond just working with clients.

MICHEL'S STORY: A MASSAGE THERAPIST TRANSITIONS TO BECOMING A PROFESSIONAL HYPNOTIST

Michael had a thriving massage therapy practice – but he wanted more. He enjoyed working with people who have a history of trauma like combat, childhood abuse, sexual abuse and/or physical abuse. His ideal client is the client who is ready to take back control of their life and begin to create a more fulfilling existence for themselves and those they love.

Here's his story:

"My hypnosis practice is so much bigger than I thought it would be, way bigger. I knew I would be helping everyday people with everyday issues, and I am. However, I have also found myself getting paid for speaking about hypnosis, writing about hypnosis for a local newspaper, being published in professional hypnosis journals as well as several online publications, mentoring new hypnotists and even creating my own hypnotic business products for other hypnosis professionals. This is not a career it is a passion and I am so glad that I found the right teacher for me because without the initial tools I'd not been able to do what I do."

"The professional hypnosis community is amazing. After

almost fifteen years as a MT in private practice I had never been able to build a support network of like-minded professionals whom I could share ideas or concerns with and well the massage therapy conventions were dismal. It seemed as if most MT's viewed fellow MT's as competition rather than resources and although that does exist in hypnosis it is extremely rare. If I had known about hypnosis and the amazing community of healers it houses I would have made the switch years earlier."

6. NOT DOING THEIR OWN INTERNAL WORK

This is the most critical element of being a world-class professional hypnotist.

It's *easier* to focus on client's issues and ignore our own.

It's *easier* to tell ourselves we need to update the website, or make a few phone calls, rather than doing our daily practice of self-hypnosis.

It's more *fun* to stay up late and watch our favorite show, than go to bed early and get the rest we need.

It's enjoyable to eat the unhealthy foods and drink, then pay for it later. And yet who is really paying?

We are. Our business is, our clients are.

As hypnotists make choices to not resolve their own internal struggles, they are not showing up fully for their clients.

For us to be the best we can be, we must do our own internal work.

Feel confident in our own abilities.

Be diligent in our practice.

Do our self-hypnosis daily.

Take personal responsibility in making our practice a success.

Be *curious* about what's happening, and be *interested* in the mind, how it works, and our own transformation. This easily translates to being curious and interested in what's going on with our clients.

Be curious about the problem state, and what is keeping it alive, it's not to be ignored, or discarded – but asked – why are you here – what is keeping you alive (in me or my client)?

Professional Hypnotist Truth #23: Being curious and interested in our client's problem helps us connect with clients and get results.

Be curious about your client's issues, and your own. Ask yourself, "I wonder how this problem is continuing to exist in my client?"
Be *interested* in how this issue is *serving* your client. There is a reason for it to continue, and if the reason is ignored or discarded, there will be resistance. One of the best questions to ask, is "If there is one good thing about keeping this issue, what would it be?"

Eat healthy, sleep well, resolve our own emotional issues.

Know that this profession changes lives! And we are *not* in competition with anyone or anything. We all have our own ideal clients that we serve. We all are the best hypnotist – for some clients.

This does not mean we have a perfect life. Far from it.

Our families suffer, and we can't "fix" them. They have to *want* the help. This can be heartbreaking.

We'll more clearly see the daily struggle in humanity and want to scream from the top of our lungs "I know I can help you!!", yet they won't believe in themselves enough to do so every time.

We'll feel tired, anxious, scared, alone, sad.

Use hypnosis to bring yourself to 100 percent.

Without using your own tools to be the best you can be, how can you expect your clients to do the same?

The next chapter brings everything full circle. I'm glad you're still here. This means you're likely *exactly the right person to become a world-class hypnotist and use hypnosis in your practice.*

CHAPTER EIGHT

GET STARTED NOW

"Find the Light in your clients.... Help them remember who they truly are. Eternal, loving, and light filled beings. The rest - the hypnosis, is easy."

– ERIKA FLINT

After helping thousands of clients with hypnosis, and over a hundred compassionate humans become hypnotists, I believe it all comes down to a few things.

Two Things

Whenever you don't know what to do, or feel anxious or stressed or are thinking or feeling anything you don't want to feel:

- **Breathe.** It is our connection to life. Breathe in life-giving oxygen. In between one breath, and the exhalation of another exists infinite possibility. Notice the feeling of your breath rising, your body lifting, and allow yourself to become captivated by the pause at the top of your breath. Relax your neck, and jaw. Be present. In that moment you are filled with expansive energy. Surrender yourself and allow the greatness of who you are — whether that be Source, Spirit, God, or Love, fill you completely.

- **Be Grateful**. I once heard that gratitude is the closest feeling to God. I've often wondered about that. Why gratitude? Why not love? Because God IS love, and the next closest thing, is gratitude. It's an action: purposefully thinking of things to be grateful for. The act of being grateful fills you with the feeling of BEING LOVE. For in that moment while you are thankful you are in a receptive mode of expansiveness and possibility.

The Ultimate Goal of a Professional Hypnotist

Our greatest goal as hypnotists, is to re-mind our clients of who they really are, of their own divinity. That they have everything they need inside of them already.

Our goal is to find the light in them. Find the spark, the life-force-energy, that creative essence that makes them *feel alive*. Then help them discard everything that is *not that*.

Hypnosis is a return to your true self. It's not a becoming, it's a remembering.

Resistance, fear, and past experience — and the lower functioning elements of the human mind, are holding us back from being our best self. Hypnosis can be used to remove all resistance, eliminate unnecessary and erroneous fear, and reframe past failures as learning opportunities. It is the life essence in our clients that we want to harness, that we want to *re*-mind them of.

Our job as hypnotists, is to find the **Light** in our clients. In many it has been lost, covered up, or buried.

Professional Hypnotist Truth #24: Look for the light in your clients. When you find it, help them associate to that light. Then remove everything else that is not the light.

The light is their life force, the creative purpose, the reason for existence. Finding that, and re-igniting it will *solve all of your clients perceived issues.*

Then help them discard everything else.

Doing This Work Is an Honor

It is a great honor to help people with some of the most difficult situations in their lives, and as you can tell from the stories in this book, it's not easy work. It's fulfilling work.

It takes daily practice, focus, courage, and the willingness to go there first — where our clients are scared and let them know it is safe to embark on the journey with you because you have been there. You know what you're doing.

You know how to navigate the dark path, and you know how to illuminate it as well.

This is not a job, but truly a calling. *Being a hypnotist is not work; it is love put into practice.*

Please consider joining me on this journey. The world needs more great hypnotists.

I hope to see you in the hypnosis classroom, and we'll explore the expansion of human consciousness together.

I need help, there's so much wonderful work to be done together.

If my words inspired you, please let me know.

With love,
Erika

Acknowledgements

To all of my clients, students, and grads who have trusted in me to help you in your own journeys of transformation and success. Thank you for allowing me to share your stories in part, and whole to help others. Thank you for being courageous and wanting more and the willingness to step into the unknown to get a better life for yourself and your families and communities.

In this book I've drawn from ideas from many fields and specialists and combined together to help people who are interested in a better understanding and expansion of human consciousness and using hypnosis to achieve our best selves *on purpose*. I've learned so much from the following colleagues and leaders whose ideas are represented in this book, arranged in my own way to reach those who resonate with my message. To Cal Banyan for your wisdom and guidance on the principles of hypnosis and 5-PATH® and 7th Path Self-Hypnosis® and the importance of having a systematic approach to hypnosis, I am forever grateful. To John Overdurf for your work on hypnosis and leading-edge neuroscience, and how it all plays the most beautiful and engaging music we call perception and consciousness, thank you for helping me expand my own awareness and share it with others. To Angela Lauria, thank you for helping me step into my future self over and over again, and especially your guidance on focusing on loving my students and getting them results, and the creation of the original idea for this book.

To my wonderful growing team at Cascade Hypnosis Center, thank you for your commitment to delivering world-class hypnosis sessions and training: Shannon Wallace, Timothy Freeman, Terra Johnston.

To my loving family for your ongoing support and encouragement of my work, my parents Will and Geri Flint, and my sisters Holly, Lindsey, and Cherish.

To the Author Incubator, my editors, and publisher, thank you for believing in me and my book and helping me create the best message to bring more light to the world.

To other supporting colleagues and friends who provided help and guidance during the creation of this book: Majeed Mogharreban, Gina Catalano, Laura Abernathy, Karen Stultz, Pam Prior, Shannon Wallace, Donna Bloom, Lawrence Winnerman, Melissa Tiers, Ron Wilder, Anthony Gitch, Christian Skoorsmith, Brian McCartney, Cherish Flint, and my personal fitness Nicola Mann who helped me flush out ideas in this book with during our 6 am training sessions.

To Paige, for your ongoing love, support and encouragement and for sharing the joy of life with me in the process.

About the Author

Erika Flint is an award-winning hypnotist and hypnotherapy instructor, best-selling author, speaker, and a co-host of the popular podcast series *Hypnosis, Etc.* She is the founder of Cascade Hypnosis Center for Training and Services in Bellingham, WA, and the creator of the *Reprogram Your Weight* system of lasting weight loss without the struggle.

Before becoming a hypnotist, Erika designed software for the high-tech industry. She worked in that field for over a decade when she realized how interested she was in the most powerful

computing device available – the human mind. Now she combines her analytical expertise along with powerful hypnosis techniques to train some of the best hypnotists in the world with a modern, systematic approach to hypnosis.

Her unique design and approach help compassionate individuals become full-time hypnotists with thriving and lucrative practices that bring meaning and purpose to their lives and relief to their communities.

Erika's heartfelt approach is the trademark of her work. She values authentic connections with people and works to re-mind others of their own divinity.

She lives in Bellingham, Washington with her family including two sweet cats and a happy rescue dog named Harlund who loves to play soccer.

Thank You

Thank you for reading this book. It is my great honor and pleasure to share this information with you in hopes that you are inspired to help bring hope and relief to the world with powerful, modern, and professional hypnosis.

I sincerely hope you are inspired and excited to embark upon a new journey in your life, one where you take your compassion for others and combine it with expertise in hypnosis to transform lives for the better – starting with your own.

My success comes from my graduates' success.

My success comes from the success of my clients and graduates. I am highly invested in ensuring my graduates become successful hypnotists with thriving practices.

If you want to become a professional hypnotist and have a lucrative and fulfilling career helping others, congratulations. You are in the right place.

I hope this book has helped you realize that you don't need an advanced degree to become a great hypnotist. All you need to start with is compassion and drive. From there, get great training to build a foundation for excellent hypnosis.

You don't need to have all your own issues figured out. The best hypnotists will become true believers in hypnosis and have their own transformation – sometimes during their training course!

HOW TO SELECT A HYPNOSIS SCHOOL

The foundation of becoming a great hypnotist begins with excellent hypnosis training, here's what to look for in a hypnosis school:

- A systematic approach to hypnosis that allows and supports students in being successful right away.
- The instructor should be an experienced and successful hypnotist, and should still be seeing private clients.
- Lots of supervised practice time during the training course.
- Excellent ongoing support.

The training program at our center focuses on the above with the intent of helping our graduates go from classroom to client immediately after graduation. I want my graduates to see clients right away and get a return on their initial training investment to grow their hypnosis practice rapidly.

I'm looking for compassionate humans who want to become world class hypnotists.

I'm looking for compassionate humans with hearts that are willing, with *Ruthless Compassion* to do the work to help their clients with hypnosis – even when everything else has failed.

Won't you join me?

Together we can make a difference. We can help the lonely, the anxious, the fearful.

Join me and be part of the solution. I can't wait to meet you and help your dreams come true.

If this book and my words and stories have inspired you, then take the next step.

The next step is to take my online masterclass called *Can You Be a Hypnotist*, at **CanYouBeAHypnotist.com.**

The ninety-minute masterclass is designed to help you know if training with me is the right option for you.

If it is, then I encourage you to apply to train with me. You can apply at CascadeHypnosisTraining.com/apply.

Additional resources mentioned in this book can be found at **CanYouBeAHypnotist.com.**

Thank You

I look forward to hearing from you, and hopefully seeing you in the classroom soon. Until then, be well and take good care of yourself. The world needs your love and compassion.

Let's help more people with the power of hypnosis.

With love,
Erika

Made in the USA
Coppell, TX
10 April 2022

76332966R10104